The Lost Covenant of the Kingdom

The Lost Covenant of the Kingdom

Rediscover the Ancient Blessings Awaiting You

Lornah Stump Nelson

Trilogy Christian Publishers A Wholly Owned Subsidiary of Trinity Broadcasting Network 2442 Michelle Drive Tustin, CA 92780

Rights Department, 2442 Michelle Drive, Tustin, CA 92780.

Trilogy Christian Publishing/ TBN and colophon are trademarks of Trinity Broadcasting Network.

For information about special discounts for bulk purchases, please contact Trilogy Christian Publishing.

Manufactured in the United States of America

10 9 8 7 6 5 4 3 2 1

Library of Congress Cataloging-in-Publication Data is available.

B-ISBN#: 978-1-64773-554-8

E-ISBN#: 978-1-64773-555-5

DEDICATION

To my covenant-keeping husband, the Lord Jesus Christ

To God, my covenant-keeping Father

To Holy Spirit, my guarantee and pledge of the
Covenant Inheritances

ACKNOWLEDGMENTS

My deep appreciation to all those that have helped me climb this mountain, for all the influencers, contributors, encouragers, and prayer partners. Thank you! I did not write this book alone. It took all of us to make it happen.

To my family--my daughter Heidi, who has always believed, encouraged, and fought for me. You have enriched my life more than you will ever know. To my son-in-law Randy, who unconditionally accepted me as part of his family, and to my amazing grandkids, Cameron, and Alyssa, Brianna, and Shaylee, you are my greatest treasures! To my sister, Sharon, thank you for your great ideas.

To Grant, how can I thank you enough for supporting me emotionally, financially, and in every other way, as well as for your enduring patience and understanding during long days and late nights of writing? Your help with grammar corrections and editing was a tremendous help. I am forever grateful!

To Susan Brooks, my loyal, faithful friend. You have been unrelenting to always believe in me and call me back to who I really am if I start to lose myself. You have encouraged me to release my giftings and have consistently prayed for me and inspired me with your prophetic words. I appreciate your policing me to get this book done. I needed that.

To Michele Witz, my BFF who has taught me so much, always inspiring me to come up higher.

To my bible study angels, Cheri Weldy, my second editor, Kathy MacKenzie with a "K," Cathy Riley, Isabele Johnson, Diane Murray aka Giggles, Sue Leslie, and all who have given me so much joy, inspiration, and love, and have continually prayed for me. You are the best!

To Donnie McNamara, my faithful beyond generous friend, who made me laugh and always knew what I needed. I will never forget.

To the late Jim Warren, my great friend who was always there encouraging me to get this done. You are missed!

INTRODUCTION

In the 1989 movie *Field of Dreams*, Ray Kinsella heard the voice, *"If you build it; He will come."* After building it, Ray says, "I have just created something totally illogical. Am I completely nuts? Until I heard the voice, I'd never done a crazy thing in my whole life. Sometimes you have no idea why... You just have to. For me it's like a dream come true."

Then later Ray's father, John Kinsella, asks him, "Is this heaven?"

To which Ray questions, "Is there a heaven?"

"Oh yeah!" John says, "Heaven is the place where dreams come true."

Ray's eyes lit up. He smiles, saying, "Maybe, this is heaven." [1]

Twenty some years after this movie, I was minding my own business when I heard the voice, *"If you build it, He will come."* It shook me to my core. I thought God may be messing with a dream that I was trying to ignore. It had felt like I was completely nuts to think about writing a book of my revelations about the lost covenant. Why so? Perhaps fear or second guessing myself had kept me from doing it. But like Ray, I couldn't ignore the voice either, so to be sure the voice was God, I put out a Gideon fleece with a time frame. I said, "Lord, if this is really you, I want you to show me this old *Field of Dreams* movie today."

When I logged on to the Internet, guess what happened? There on my screen was a high-lighted article about this movie, and that night, there it was on my TV. Obviously, it was time to begin my journey. Like Ray Kinsella, I had no idea why I was chosen to fulfill this dream. I just knew I had to. John Kinsella was right; heaven is the place where dreams come true. It's about heaven invading earth to bring the dream to pass, so that it can be a blessing to others. A fulfilled dream is indeed a little piece of heaven on earth, especially when it is destined by divine design.

The fulfillment of my dream has been several years in the making. About seventeen of them were spent learning, preparing, receiving revelation, taking notes, doing research, experiencing changes, and sharing it with others. Writing the book took another five years.

During these years, all hell seemed to come against me in the forms of strong opposition and hard situations. At times, I found myself overpowered--down for the count, if you will. Amid the onslaught of resistances, I began thinking that my dream would never become a reality. It was taking way too long and seemed too hard to do. Satan, the dream stealer, had moved in to steal my dreams.

Like King David in Psalm 18, NKJV, "In my distress, I called upon the Lord. He heard my cry and bowed the heavens and came down. He drew me out of many waters and delivered me from my enemies that were too strong for me." When all appeared hopeless, God Himself came down to rescue me and to resurrect my dreams. Wow! It was the architect and builder of dreams that helped me catch hold of them, to dream again.

Dream Catcher, did you notice that you can't do this alone? It takes God, the Dream Maker, to breathe life into your dreams to fulfill His purpose. He puts those dreams in the womb of your passion, so you will be captivated by them and not quit. You can fall again and again, but God will resurrect those passions. *If you go the distance,* it will happen! Why? Because you are God's glory, and your dreams coming true glorify Him. That's why Satan tries to steal your dreams. He not only wants to hurt you, but his goal is to actually steal the glory of God. Can you see why it is so important that you get back up? Let the God of Resurrection breathe life into what has died.

Perhaps many of you have old dreams you gave up on that should be resurrected or new ones to pursue, but you need help getting there. Learning about your covenant rights and blessings will give you a new identity with renewed hope. It is time for past disappointments to be washed away so each dream can become a reality. If you have had demonic resistances, fear, insecurities, or distractions that have hindered you from your destiny, then it is time to *"Go the distance,"* persevering one. If you build it and don't quit, God will come to empower you to finish it. No matter what comes, don't give up, and it will happen!

You are living in an energy field called the Kingdom of God; it is a field where you have unlimited potential to dream. These dreams are lit up by the strongest emotions you carry--your passions. You create the energy field for them to manifest in by what you think, believe, feel, and speak. For instance, fear, doubt, unbelief, a poverty mindset, depression, etc. creates the fields you don't want to live in. You can tune into the right frequency of the promised covenant inheritances and build a field of your dreams.

Negative energy is exhausting and takes the same energy as positive beliefs but without desirable results. You don't want to keep your song locked in your heart or your story unread or your business unbuilt. Others will miss out. Don't deprive them of their blessings! Just start taking small steps towards your dreams. You don't have to impact the world in one day. Just begin one step at a time and expect big results.

We all stand in the shadows of Martin Luther, who in the early 1500s had a dream, and amid great resistance, he brought back the new covenant of grace. By doing this, Martin caused a revolution and changed the world. He said, "Salvation of grace alone, through faith alone, for Christ's sake alone is the principle upon which all teachings rest."

Another world changer, Martin Luther King Jr, impacted our culture drastically right in the midst of great turmoil and grief. He said, "I have a dream where little black boys and black girls will be able to join hands with little white boys and white girls as sisters and brothers."

We all have dreams. I have a dream to see the Church walk in the birthrights, blessings, and benefits of the new covenant. I have a dream that the incredible intimacy of the covenant and the supernatural power of the kingdom will be brought together with equal importance. I have a dream to see each child of God win every battle as proof of the blessings of the blood covenant. I have a dream for a revolution of new covenant living.

David Wilkerson believed the new covenant was assigned to the end times. He alleged that it was the answer to meet all our needs and the secret to unleashing the power to do the works of Jesus in advancing His kingdom.

In Michael Galiga's book, *Win Every Battle,* he says, "If you learn to live in covenant and in intimacy with God, there is no devil or demon powerful enough to stop His supernatural intervention in your life. No plot or plan of the enemy can stop you from winning every battle. It's impossible to win every battle unless you're in covenant with Him." [2]

Jon and Joline Hamil said, "Before the third Great Awakening can happen, we must return to the Covenant." [3]

Sean Feucht believes "Covenant is the bedrock for the coming wave of God to land on. It is the key to unlock cities and nations." [4]

Editor Julie Smith of the Elijahlist recognized that "Covenant will sustain the next great move" [5] and challenged writers to write and teach the profound revelation of covenant that we need to learn to walk in.

Chuck Pierce prophesied, "God was going to cause a rebuilding process; to loose an apostolic rebuilding. That which had been built on religious spirits, will no longer be part of the believer. God is going to rebuild and cause a blueprint from Heaven to come down; the building plan for the future. It will happen suddenly and change some old religious minds. Suddenly, God will break the spirit of poverty off and we are going to arise and build that which is built in Heaven. Now is the time it will begin to be manifest in the earth." [6] Build it and He will come!

I believe the *Lost Covenant of the Kingdom* is a blueprint to build your future. It will provide the rebuilding process that will turn you from old religious mindsets that keep you bound to a new identity of freedom and blessings through the New Covenant.

Our website, thelostcovenant.com, will contain curriculum and short videos to make sure you acquire a greater understanding of how to live in covenant. Then you will be able to teach your friends, associates, neighbors, small groups, business gatherings, or church groups. This site will allow you to connect and glean from the experiences of one another. Together we will build a great network of covenant keepers.

It is time to have a REVOLUTION of covenant living!

Welcome to the REVOLUTION!

WARNING!

The Introduction is a harbinger (a forerunner) to the book. If you didn't read it, please go back to do so. Then begin your adventurous journey to discover the treasures awaiting you, starting with "Chapter One: Why Was I Ever Born?"

TABLE OF CONTENTS

CHAPTER 1 – WHY WAS I EVER BORN?

The two most important days in a man's life is the day he was born and the day he discovers why.

--Mark Twain

Do you know why you're here on the earth? The day of your *birth* and the day you discover *why* you were born are the two most significant days of your life. Why so? Check out what Mr. Purpose, Rick Warren, says, "The greatest tragedy in life is not death, but life without purpose." [7] And Dr. Myles Munroe adds, "It is dangerous to be alive and not know why you were given life. Wherever purpose is not known, 'abuse' is inevitable." [8] OK, so how might this relate to you?

The word abuse (ab/use) can mean "abnormal use" or "to misuse." [9] Living your life differently from the original purpose and design would be *miss*-using the life you were given. That's right! God planned your life long before your birth, and it's about the who and why: *who* God is for you and *who* He says you are; *why* you were born and *why* you are here now. And guess what? If you don't know God, your identity, and your purpose of birth, your life won't be as it should be--the way it was meant to be, according to God's magnificent design. Case in point, take a look at the nurse mare's foal.

A Nurse Mare's Foal

After eleven months of pregnancy, the nurse mare lays down. She is restless as she gets up, then down repetitively for hours. Sweating profusely, she begins the hard heavy labor as her water breaks. The nurse mare writhes on the ground as first a leg pops out, then the head. After about an hour of struggle, the foal is born. The worn out mare needs a few minutes rest until she can stand up to lick and clean her foal. By nuzzling her newborn, she actually helps it stand up. The beauty of the bonding process has begun. The splendor of God's design is shown in all its glory.

But wait! This foal will be taken away from its mother and thrown out into a field, left to die as an unwanted cast away. What! How can this be? Sadly, this is the fate of the foal from a nurse mare. The reason for this foal's birth is to bring its mother into milk so she can nourish not her own foal, but a more expensive one: a purebred. The nurse mare's purpose is to suckle the privileged colt of a thorough-bred while its mother is sent away each year to be re-bred. (See borntodie.org)

The foals from these nurse mares are byproducts of thoroughbred racing. They are born to die. Without a pedigree, these foals have no worth because they can never make the kind of money that purebreds would. Unwanted and rejected, they are referred to as "junk mares," (good for nothing trash) and like trash, they are destroyed. Dr. Myles Munroe was spot on.

Misunderstanding the purpose of any birth can cause tremendous abuse, pain, and even death. Is this what God intended? Jeremiah 29:11 (ESV) tells of God's plans for us:

I know the plans [purpose] I have [designed] for you, declares the LORD, plans for welfare [peace, safety, prosperity, health and wholeness]; and not for evil [calamity, distress, misery, injury, or disease] to give you a future and a hope.[10]

This hope is one you long for with the expected successful outcome promised to the righteous.

Suffering happens to everyone at times, but *unnecessary* heartache and pain can result by living in opposition to God's design for your life. Bill Johnson says, "Sin is simply anything that violates God's original design."[11] You were meant to live in God's designed plans within the Jeremiah covenant blessings of peace, safety, prosperity, health, and wholeness. But don't worry. God has offered you a covenant with His Son that enables you to fulfill Jeremiah 29:11.

For many years I didn't have a clue why I was born or know about my covenant with Christ. What about you? What's your story? Do you know why on earth you're here? Who you really are? Have you ever felt like a nurse mare's foal: unwanted, rejected, and underestimated in value? Were you sometimes a byproduct of other people's dysfunction and selfishness, or your own?

Some of us were devalued from birth. That was my story. I wasn't wanted. In fact, my parents tried to abort me but obviously failed. I was an unwanted castaway, and some of the chapters in my life sucked and not all of them were good. But guess what? I'm no longer like a poor "junk mare." Because of our covenant, God has clothed me in His splendor and made me beautiful. (see Ezekiel 16:14, TLB)

I've been set free from the torment of rejection and the shame of never being good enough. This transformation was actually recorded by Ezekiel in the Bible. Imagine that! I didn't know it, but God was at my birth. Heaven celebrated me. But now I want you to think on this! God rejoiced over you too. Ezekiel was really telling about what God wanted to do for all of His covenant partners and especially for the hurting or unwanted. Could this be your story too?

Ezekiel's Prophetic Words

> On the day you were born, no one cared about you. No one had the slightest interest in you; no one pitied you or cared for you. On that day when you were born, you

were unwanted, dumped in a field and left to die. But I [God] came by and saw you there, helplessly kicking about in your own blood. As you lay there, I said, 'Live!' And I helped you to thrive like a plant in the field! You grew up and became a beautiful jewel. Your breasts became full, and your body hair grew, but you were still naked [in shame].

And when I passed by again, I saw that you were old enough for love. So I wrapped my cloak around you to cover your nakedness and declared my marriage vows. I made a covenant with you, says the Sovereign LORD, and you became mine. I gave you expensive clothing of fine linen and silk, beautifully embroidered, and sandals made of fine goatskin leather. I gave you lovely jewelry, bracelets, beautiful necklaces, a ring for your nose, earrings for your ears, and a lovely crown for your head. And so you were adorned with gold and silver... You ate the finest foods—choice flour, honey, and olive oil--and became more beautiful than ever. You looked like a queen, and so you were! Your fame soon spread throughout the world because of your beauty. I dressed you in my splendor and perfected your beauty, says the Sovereign LORD.

--Ezekiel 16:4a, 58, 10-14, NLT

Did you know that a covenant with God was this stunning, this magnificent? It's all about God's extreme generosity to His covenant partners--those men and women He makes into kings and queens and the unwanted junk mares He makes into Triple Crown winners. This covenant was intended to enrich your life and rewrite your story so you can go from a normal life to a supernatural one, from who you once were to who you really are in Christ. By discovering God, you discover yourself as He summons you into your potential. Yes, this seems too good to be true. I thought so too until God gave me purpose and began perfecting my beauty.

CHAPTER 2 – MY STORY

When your negative past calls you, don't answer. It has nothing new to say.

--Author Unknown

What About My Past?

God did make me beautiful, but let's talk turkey here. It wasn't always like that. In the past, there were chapters where I wanted to die more than live. I really didn't want to take my life. I just wanted to escape the emptiness and loneliness I felt and to somehow disappear or cease to exist.

Growing up was too hard at times and intensely painful. Life seemed hopeless, and I felt helpless to change it. I didn't like myself or the person I had become--so needy, lonely, and insecure. A battle was going on in my soul: Who was I? What was wrong with me? And why was I ever born?

My young friends had hopeful dreams as they primped and practiced singing or dancing in front of a mirror. I was in front of a mirror too, but I had no dreams. My "mirror on the wall" made me cry. It always told me I was the unfairest of them all, and that I didn't have what it took to be loved. I was a mere teen, sixteen to be exact. I just longed to be loved, as well as to have someone define me and tell me I was pretty. My highest hope was that I would someday marry a man who would love me and stay faithful to that love. My greatest fear was that he wouldn't. Yes, I thought I was a mistake and horribly flawed. Oh, how I wanted to escape the shame and depression of never being enough.

My father's alcoholic rages made me stay in my room, afraid to speak to him. He despised me. Those frequent words *"You're no good and you'll never be any good"* stung worse than bees squished between my toes. Was I that bad? Mom and my only sibling usually had to pull Dad off me to stop his beatings and protect my life by sneaking me out to a motel until he sobered up.

When Mom compared me to my older sister, she would say, *"Why can't you do anything right?"* I didn't know the answer to that. No matter how hard I tried, it was never enough. Her disapproval cut sharp like a knife. Apparently it was I, the second born, who was the problematic outcast, and never my sister. What had I done? I was clueless until many years later when I found out that Dad thought I was another man's child. Even so, my question went unanswered: "why was I born?"

The Prison of the Past

My parents were victims of their own dysfunctional home lives, which they passed on to me as my sense of normal. My father was cruelly abusive just like his father; yet, Dad was a "chick magnet," a handsome playboy who attracted women like flies. His infidelities, betrayals, and lies were normal parts of our lives. I hated this about him; yet, somehow, I ended up continuing in it.

I didn't know that our pasts could become prisons that perpetuated the bondage of those who raised us. Held captive by others wrongs, we could become victimized and then could unintentionally reproduce the same destructive culture in ourselves or those around us. That was because victims live by fear.

Did you know that unresolved fears can attract the very things you don't want? Like attracts like. "What I feared has come upon me; what I dreaded has happened to me" (Job 3:25, NIV). Fear involves a punishment that matches the fear (see 1 John 4:18, NIV). For instance, my fear of betrayal drew the betrayers to me. Fear is not from God. He said, "Fear not" some 365 times, one for every day. That's because fear can sabotage you where you end up with what you feared--that which causes you much pain.

Yep, you heard right. Some little girls grow up to marry men like their fathers with the traits they fear and detest. That was what I did. Without realizing it, my choices recreated what I grew up with. I didn't know how to lay down the familiar. Perhaps it was too frightening to leave the certainty of the known for the unknown when a family-spirit was familiar. Could this be why I married?

My Mess Ups

It was easy for me to marry. I had multiple offers from good-looking playboys like my dad. I was attracted to bad boys, and familiar spirits seem to find each other. These pretty boys wanted a trophy wife, and I "fit the bill" when I became Miss Pepsi Cola and a model for Catalina swimwear. Even though others found me attractive, I was surprised by all the attention. I felt ugly at times.

It was the dashing good looks of my suitors that proved to me I must have value. So what if they had a lifestyle of infidelity and dishonesty? The fact that someone this handsome wanted me above all others gave me hope that I could be a "thoroughbred." I wanted to be a trophy wife. That meant I was pretty. For a little while I was special, maybe even loved. A marriage would follow, then betrayals, lies, and divorce. It seemed to be the American way, at least in Southern California where it was common to have several marriages. Our motto was really crazy: "If it doesn't work, just try it again."

I didn't sleep around; I married around to appease my conscience about sex outside of marriage. I thought he would settle down and change, that my love would be enough. It never was. Eventually a seductress would show up. Attracted by his impressive looks and familiar spirit, she would seduce him by appealing to his vanity and playboy propensities. He couldn't resist. He was a prisoner of his past, but so was I. Both of us were broken and had no idea how to get fixed.

The infidelities, lies, and lack of repentance hurt bitterly. Divorce seemed my only option, but I dreaded being alone. Fear and loneliness would overtake me; yet, somehow, another handsome womanizer would show up to help me in my neediness. Like the cat that chases her tail in circles, I had a cycle of striking out, then marrying again the same way but expecting different results. Behavior like this, they say, is insanity. Yes, I was insane, trapped in craziness I couldn't escape.

Three strikes and I was out. I had reached the end of my thirties, and I was done. But how could I stop this cyclic lifestyle? I had no clue how to change, but I had questions, like, "Is this all there is to life? Does God really exist? And if so, does He care about me? Am I fixable?"

From Whining to Winning

I needed answers. I was more than desperate, and I was tired of the life I knew. My life had to change, or else I didn't want to go on. In despair, I visited a church. Tears ran down my face as I cried out to the One I hoped existed, "God, if you're real, take over my life and change me. Please."

God did hear my feeble attempt. He was real! Without condemnation, He loved me right then and there. It felt like hot oil oozing over me as every ounce of my being came alive. My heart raced; my breathing deepened, and then there was utter calm and total peace. I had never felt such feelings.

This was a defining moment, a sudden life-altering encounter coming to me from another realm as my story was radically interrupted. I was no longer alone! God was present in my reality, and He wanted me to give all of myself to Him, including the negative, the bad, and the ugly. As I did, a cocoon of hope enveloped me. Things seemed different. I was different inside, as well as deeply and powerfully touched.

This God of love began to answer all my questions, especially the big one: "why was I born?" My birth did have purpose! Suddenly, I had hope for my future. Bill Johnson said, "Purpose is future and you need to know you have one." [12] At fortyish, I began to find my destiny, and my life was profusely enriched, so much so, that I couldn't keep it to myself. This was just too good! I wanted you in on it so you could see the purpose of your birth. Unique to each individual is a *personal* purpose (what you're assigned to do), but also available to everyone are identical *corporate* destinies. So this discovery was for you too.

In a nutshell, you were born to have intimacy with God, then to discover your identity and fulfill your purpose or destiny. God chose a life for you made in heaven. I know this seems too good to be true, but beloved, it is true! Your past doesn't have to dictate your future. God will unplug you from it and rewire you for a new future. Mark Chironna says, "God doesn't have a plan for your life; He has a purpose, and He has hundreds of plans to get you to your purpose." [13]

Jesus has already made you His champion with a Triple Crown win. That's who you really are. It's how He sees you. You were meant to live in God's image and reflect His incredible beauty by fulfilling your divine destiny, the purpose for your birth. Even if you don't yet know why you were born, beautiful one, you can relax. I have really good news for you. The answer is on its way, and here's a clue.

The purpose of your birth is tied up in the mystery of Christ's birth. There is a secret surrounding this birth that has the power to completely rock your world, where you will never be the same. When you understand this, you will be able to walk into the destiny meant for all of God's children and live it out by God's brilliant design. This secret was meant to be discovered by you.

Your life will still have challenges to overcome but if it isn't glorious, miraculous, astonishing and absolutely incredible at the same time, then you are missing God's plan for your birth. Are you ready to have your thinking remodeled and revolutionized for results that will astound you?

CHAPTER 3– THE PURPOSE OF YOUR BIRTH

Your life has purpose. Your story is important. Your dreams count. Your voice matters. You were born to make an impact.

--Author Unknown

The Purpose of Christ's Birth

I happened to stumble upon an amazing discovery about the birth of Christ when I was asked to speak at a Christian women's conference during the Christmas season. I wanted God to give me a deeper revelation of His birth, something different than the amazing story of the bright star filled sky of angels, the shepherds, the wise men, and the manger scene that we all know and love so much. My desire was to present insight that was beyond the familiar story. I had no idea this would turn my life upside down then right side up, upgrading it, not just in part, but with a whole new life!

My Christmas request had an immediate response. Presented to me in my mind was a question that was profound and thought provoking. For the first time, I wondered why Jesus came as a baby and not as an adult. Adam came to earth as an adult. God and the pre-incarnate Christ appeared to some patriarchs in the form of a man in various theophanies of the Old Testament. (see Genesis 18:1-3.) Even angels came to earth as men and still do to this day. Suddenly, Christ's birth became something to be explored, perhaps a mystery yet to be disclosed.

As I focused on why God had to be born as a baby, my perspective took a quantum leap. I saw the purpose for all of our births. *Oh em gee*! This far exceeded any expectations I've ever had. It was thrilling beyond words! Now I want you to know too, dear destined one, what a great purpose you have been given by God. What you will read has the definite possibility to drastically change your life and rewrite your story to a life of the miraculous. Are you ready for this dynamic upgrade?

My Journey to Find the Answers

I thought I knew the answer to this reflective and puzzling question of why a baby instead of a man.

"Well Lord," I said. "Jesus was born as a baby to identify with humanity and to pay for the sins of mankind yet be sinless."

Of course, this was true, very true. But then other thoughts immediately crossed my mind. Adam started the human race as an adult, and yet he identified with humanity extremely well. In fact, Adam started out sinless. So then why couldn't Jesus, the Last Adam, enter earth as an adult and relate with mankind while maintaining His purity to atone for sin? Obviously, He could have.

I hadn't yet grasped the mystery of this birth. I wanted to know the answer, so I thought hard on it. *OK*, I thought to myself. *Let's try this*. "Jesus was born to bring the kingdom of God and reveal His perfect Father to a broken humanity. As King of the Jews, He was born to die on a cross, not as a king but like the castaway of a nurse male's foal to save humanity from the kingdom of darkness. He was born to destroy the evil works of the devil by giving His Holy Spirit to the Church." Surely, the answer was one of these?

As I thought on the absolute truths of these statements, I heard in my spirit, "All of these were accomplished by Jesus as an adult: the revealing of the Father and His kingdom; the finished work of the cross; the devil's defeat and the gift of the Holy Spirit. In fact, His ministry didn't start until He was an adult."

Again the question was proposed to me in my mind, "So then why did Jesus need to come to earth as a baby, instead of an adult?"

I had not yet answered the question. Now I was completely puzzled. Struggling, I came up with one more try of another truth.

"He was born to fulfill the prophecies about His birth," I said with confidence. And how true that was! Of course, all of God's prophecies must be realized, and they were, but this hadn't answered *why* Jesus had to be born as a baby, only that He would be.

His appearance on earth as an infant, even with these prophetic predictions, caused many of the Jews to reject their Messiah because they expected Him to appear as a king from heaven. There seemed to be a big secret that surrounded this birth. God had my utmost attention.

The Answer: Why Was Jesus Christ Born?

I knew I was about to know why and see something that I had never thought about before. My search immediately took me to the prophetic words of Isaiah:

> For to us a *child is born*, to us *a son is given*, [assigned] and the government will be on his shoulders. Of the increase of his government and peace there will be no end. He will reign on David's throne and over his kingdom, establishing and upholding it with justice [God's law] and righteousness [what God calls right; the way it should be] from that time on and forever.
>
> --Isaiah 9:6-7, ESV

God seemed to breathe on a few words as clues when some stood out like flashing lights. They were "*child is born*" and "*son is given,*" so, I looked up the meaning of each word. "Child" in Hebrew means "a boy child." In Greek, "child" means "infant." This is similar to Matthew 2:9 where the star stopped over the place where the [infant boy] child was.

"Son" in Hebrew means "anointed or appointed one." In Greek, "son" means "sharing the father's nature and heir with legal right to the father's inheritance and estate." This is seen in John 3:16 (NKJV), "For God so loved the world that He gave His only begotten Son [heir] ."[14]

Isaiah had prophesied that a male infant (Jesus) would be born from the womb of a woman. He was God's Son (Christ), the legal heir to His Father's inheritance and estate. As an adult, Jesus would be appointed and anointed to bring His Father's governmental kingdom to earth as it is in heaven.

Jesus was born under the old covenant law of Moses. Under the law, the Hebrew's *first born* son was heir to the birthrights and the father's blessing. The inheritance usually went to the eldest son of the father, the first to burst the womb, and if he died, it passed to the *second born* son.

Suddenly I saw it! My heart raced with anticipation; my eyes opened to a magnificent brilliant plan all the way back from Adam to Jesus! Jesus being birthed was hugely about inheriting the *rights of birth* from His biological ancestors and the *blessings* from His Father, God. To qualify under the law as heir, He had to be human, born of a mother for the birthrights, and the first to burst the womb. He needed to be the *first born* Son of His Father, and in this case, His *only begotten* Son.

"*Only begotten*" was crucial so all inheritances after Jesus's death would not be passed on to the biological second born half-brother of Jesus, the son of both Joseph and Mary. The firstborn's blessings were to go to the "*begotten of God*," the *spiritual* second born, "born again" sons from Abba Father.

Friends, that includes you and me! You were begotten of God when you were born-again! (see 1 John 5: 4,18; 1 Peter 1:3, 23) Your covenant with Jesus gave you the right to inherit it all. 2 Peter 1:3 tells us that God by His power gave you absolutely everything needed for an amazing life. Woo hoo! Did you get this? This should give everyone gargantuan hope. Here's more proof.

"Worthy is the Lamb who was slain to receive power and wealth and wisdom and might and honor and glory and blessing!" (Revelation 5:12, ESV). Jesus, the Sacrificial Lamb, received all these blessings on the cross when He was slain, but why? Didn't He already possess them? Then I saw it. God, the Christ, possessed them, but not the man Jesus. The "Last Adam" hung on the cross--not *for you,* but *as you.* (see Philippians 2:7; 1 Corinthians 15:45)

His *birth* had qualified *Jesus,* the first born and only begotten heir, to receive the firstborn birthrights from Mary's lineage and the spiritual blessings from Father God. One of the reasons He had to die was so that you, the second born (born again and begotten of God), could inherit the firstborn's inheritance rights of power, wealth, wisdom, might, honor, glory, and blessing. (see Revelation 5:12)

Prior to the cross, Jesus said, "Now Father, bring me into the glory we shared before the world began" (John 17:5, NLT). As the slain human sacrifice, He re-received everything to be able to pass each one on to His kind, mankind. Christ, as God, owned everything but forfeited it all; then He re-inherited them as Jesus, a man, to be able to give you all that was lacking and everything you had need of. He was the Son of Man that you might become the sons and heirs of God through your second birth.

Included with these spiritual blessings from God were the material blessings and birth rights from the ancestors of the lineages of Mary and Joseph. Physical and spiritual blessings were put in your account so you could live life the way it should be lived. This was gigantic!

The first Adam was a living soul, but Jesus--the Last Adam--was a life-giving spirit. He was the first begotten of a new race of men to be seen on the earth who were both natural *and* spiritual, as well as mutually human *and* divine. The power on high came upon Jesus at His baptism, as yours did when you were born again. Did you get this, godly one? If you did, you will never again say, "I am only human." No, you're not *only* human if you are born again! Christ's Spirit lives in you. You are godlike, divinity in humanity. This is huge! Do you really understand this made you a new creation?

The Letter from Heaven

This revelation of the covenant inheritance was beyond life altering; it was almost incomprehensible. It was like receiving a certified letter informing you about an older brother who had died as king of a country. You, as the second born, were next to inherit unfathomable riches, rights, rank, and rule over a nation. And there was more. Even the material inheritances of his ancestors from eons back belonged to you. This letter had the power and ability within it to drastically impact the way you live; so much so, that your former existence would be unrecognizable and cease to exist.

At first, I didn't know what to do with this revelation. Prior to this, my life had been a constant struggle of trying to fit in to be accepted. As the second born in my family, I was the outcast. I was like trash, a mere junk mare, but this covenant said the second born had the means to win the race.

The covenant brought me into the royal family of God, the

King of the universe, and I was to be forever accepted and undeniably loved. This second birth made me a partaker of the kingdom of God, inheriting position, rights, and the riches of this kingdom along with authority and power to co-rule with God on earth. It made me altogether new, a thoroughbred and not ever again a junk mare.

I was undone and wrecked. This was so huge that for a while I couldn't wrap my mind around it; nor could I understand the magnitude of this covenant. It was mind blowing. The upgrade was too grand, seemingly as vast as heaven was from the earth. But it was real. Heaven had come to earth to partner with me. My guilt and struggle of missing the mark, of being inadequate, was now over.

My life was no longer to be about external circumstances shaping me. I was now a "new man," all things being made new to me. I was to partner with the Word and be in agreement with Jesus to live out *what God said* about me. It was a new mindset--the mind of Christ, to think as He thinks.

Would I believe that God said I was born again with a second birth, which made me totally a new creation and the bride of Christ? ...That I was one with the Son and *joint heirs* with Jesus? ...That this marriage covenant with Jesus, like that of a natural marriage, brought me into my Groom's family, whereby His Father became my Abba Father, and I became a child and *heir* of Father God? (see Romans 8:17)

Heir of God, do you believe that being a joint heir with Jesus and an heir of God was an extremely important part of God's original design? Jesus came to earth to unveil what belongs to you as the *second born* in the family of God and to bring you into your destined story, God's unique design written before the foundations of the world. (See 1 Peter 1:20)

God wanted to make sure that you would get where you are

supposed to go and to live your life the way it should be lived. Isaiah 48:17 (NKJV) says, "I am the Lord your God who teaches you to profit, who leads you in the way you should go." God made plans to fulfill the purpose of your birth. He did it by planning your end first (a successful outcome) then backed up to begin your beginning so that somewhere in your future, you would catch up to your predestined purpose. Oh yeah! That's right.

Isaiah prophesied it:

> Remember the former things of old For I am God... Declaring the end from the beginning, And from ancient times the things that are not yet done... Indeed I have spoken it, I will also bring it to pass, I have purposed it, I will also do it.
>
> --Isaiah 46:9-11, NKJV

King David knew this. He penned, "You saw me before I was born... Every day of my life was recorded in your book. Every moment was laid out before a single day had passed." (Psalm 139:16, NLT). And loved one, God's plans for your life were pre-written too. As the second born joint heir of Jesus, you were given the inheritances of both the old and new covenants, and the promised blessings of the former and latter rains. (see Joel 2:23) "Therefore every student of the Scriptures who becomes a disciple in the kingdom of heaven is like someone who brings out new and old treasures from the storeroom" (Matt. 13:52, CEV).

Did you know that the Old Testament of ancient times (the former rains) had prophetically revealed this forthcoming New Covenant order of Jesus (the latter rains), where the second born becomes heir of the firstborn's birthrights and blessings? This new order was *concealed* within these patriarchal lineages so that you, as the second born, could *discover* your blessings.

"It is God's privilege to conceal things and the king's privilege to discover them" (Proverbs 25:2, NLT).

So straighten up your crown, royal one. It's time to go on a treasure hunt and discover the blessings that rightfully belong to you as second born heir. You were never insignificant to God. Even creation was made for you, and after it was finished, you arrived. God had great purpose for you!

CHAPTER 4 – THE NEW PROPHESIED IN THE OLD

Giving thanks to the Father, who has qualified us to be partakers of the inheritance of the saints in the light.

--Colossians 1:12 NKJV

Pulling the Ancient Blessings into Today

God had an ingenious plan to get the blessings to you. After Jesus died, His firstborn birthrights and blessings were to go to the second born (born-again). This was so significant that God prophetically illustrated it in the Old Testament. You may not know this, but it began with Abraham, the father of faith. The covenant blessings from God to him were not to be passed on to Ishmael, the firstborn son, according to the law. The second born son Isaac, the child of promise, was the heir. The blessing then went from Isaac to Jacob, the second born, instead of Esau, the firstborn.

Jacob's son Joseph had two sons, Ephraim and Manasseh, but Jacob under the Spirit of prophecy purposely crossed his hands to bless second-born Ephraim with the firstborn's birthright. And Judah, another son of Jacob, had twins; however, the *second* twin, Perez, received the blessings instead of Zerah, the one who made his appearance first and had been designated as the firstborn heir. Then there was David's son, Solomon, made heir to the throne, who was his second born in Jerusalem and Bathsheba's second child.

Could these be coincidences? I think not. God's focus was definitely on the second born. What do you think? Could these be hidden clues? Perhaps this was why God called Himself, "the God of Abraham, Isaac and Jacob" and not the God of Noah, Moses and David. The first three patriarchs were prophetic examples of Jesus' new covenant order, where the heir was the second born and the firstborn was to serve him. This was also where the inheritance of the second born was not to be shared by the first born; hence, the child of flesh would persecute the child of covenant. (see Rom 9:12; Gal 4:23)

Why Abraham, Isaac and Jacob?

Abraham had been chosen as an example of this new covenant process. I wanted to know why him? In my research, I found a potential clue in the Torah where Abram had left his father for a while to live with ancestors, Noah and Shem. Abraham was fifty-eight years old when Noah died and one hundred ten when Shem passed. He had spent many years getting instruction from the one who built the ark, the one who knew Methuselah, who in turn knew Adam. I concluded from this that Abraham had been given firsthand information about the inherited blessings since its conception in the Garden.

How could Abraham doubt the blessing? The power of covenant was "The Blessing." Abraham believed God and could be trusted, among other things, to teach his second born son to pass on the birthrights and covenant blessings to the designated heir. "For I have chosen Him [Abram] so that he will direct his children and his household after him to keep the way of the Lord" (Genesis 18:19, NIV). Did you know that if Abraham hadn't done this, all these incredible blessings meant for you would not be yours?

To protect these inheritances, the pre-incarnate Lord met with Abraham in the Old Testament to tell him about the forthcoming cross. "Your father Abraham rejoiced to see my day: and he saw it, and was glad" (John 8:56 KJV). It was to be through this cross that Christ's future born again covenant partners would be able to connect to the Old Testament promises and inherit the blessings of Abraham. Wow! What an ingenious full-proof plan!

Here's the proof:

> Therefore know that only those who are of faith are sons of Abraham. So then those who are of faith are blessed with believing Abraham. Christ redeemed us from the curse of the law, having become a curse for us (for It is written, 'Cursed is everyone who hangs on a tree'), that the blessing of Abraham might come upon the Gentiles in Jesus Christ.
>
> --Galatians 3:7, 9, 13-14, NKJV

Now that will get you shouting. Jesus took the curse so you could have the blessing of Abraham and the Lord had blessed Abraham in *everything* (see Genesis 24:1). If this is so, heir of Abraham, doesn't it make sense to find out what promised blessings were given to Abraham, Isaac, and Jacob – all the way to Jesus – and that now belong to you?

The blessing of Abraham was the generational promises of God guaranteed to Abraham's rightful heirs. Since Jesus was of the sacred lineage of Abraham, "The Blessing" was passed to Him and then to you, His covenant partner. He had taken the curse, so you could have "The Blessing."

This was huge, redeemed one! You were freed from curses because you were connected to both the Old and New Covenant blessings (the former and latter rains). Of course God did this legally. In Genesis 15:17 (KJV), God, as the Smoking Furnace, made covenant with Abraham through Christ, who was called the Burning Lamp. (More proof - Exodus 19:18, NASB; Revelation 21:22-23, ESV). This was the legal link to the old covenant blessings.

The pre-incarnate Christ had stood in proxy for Abraham while he was in a deep sleep. Abraham was able to give his permission but was probably rendered immobile so that he wouldn't mess it up or break covenant later. God had entered into an unbreakable eternal faith covenant with Abraham, and as long as Christ kept the covenant *for* Abraham, you were assured of inheriting "The Blessing."

As a result of Christ standing in for Abraham, Jesus Christ could stand in proxy for you on the cross while you were in a deep sleep in the Father's heart. Jesus died *as you* and resurrected *as you*, so you would be assured of inheriting these blessings. He kept this covenant for you by paying the price for your sins with His blood to make you forever righteous, so you couldn't break it by sinning. This new covenant made it possible for you, the recipient, to inherit all the promised blessings of Abraham.

"And if you are Christ's, then you are Abraham's seed, and heirs according to the promise" (Galatians 3:29, NKJB). Isaac and Jacob were Abraham's second born biological sons who inherited all the promises given to them and their father by God. As the second born, spiritual descendants of Jesus, you were grafted into Abraham's lineage, inheriting all promises given by God.

This was for you and your posterity; the unlimited covenant inheritances in Christ. Did you grasp the enormity of this yet? Don't take this lightly, heir of Abraham! Ought not Abraham's children be loosed from Satan's bondages? (See Luke 13:16)

"The Blessing" brings more blessings and reverses the curse of subjugation and bondage. The curse of the law is still in the world, but it is powerless through the blood. So, embrace these blessings, not according to your goodness, but because God is good. Jesus paid a hefty price on that cross for you to live forever jubilantly blessed.

What Promised Blessings of Abraham Belong to You?

Did you know that Abraham was very rich with material items such as cattle, silver, and gold? He lived long and strong in peace, honor, and prosperity because "The Lord had blessed Abraham in all things" (Genesis 24:1b, NKJV). These blessings not only enriched his life but were meant to overflow to others, all the way to you.

God had made Abraham and Sarah's name great for this reason. They were *blessed to be a blessing* and were famous for their generosity. The Torah tells us that Abraham was so rich he built inns on the main roads so wayfarers could find food and rest. He would charge them nothing, saying, "Don't thank me, thank God who has greatly blessed me." And Sarah fed women and children, taking care of them without charge and telling them, "Don't thank me, thank God who feeds and sustains all living creatures."

Their tent house was so big they had entrances on all four sides with signs saying, "All are Welcome." Each night when everyone was in bed, Sarah made clothes for the poor and needy while the glory cloud hovered over her tent. They became famous so others could find the love of God.

Beloved, did you get this? They were blessed because prosperity had a purpose. It was according to God's design. Prosperity was about entering into the fullness of God's purpose for their lives, which would give them the ability to be generous to others. Don't misunderstand God's prosperity! It's gotten a bum rap because it was misused and abused. You are blessed in His love so that you can bless others!

My dear friend, you too were meant to have the blessings of Abraham and to change the world in someone's life. Prosperity belongs to you. You were born to win and to shine! If you first focus on *being* a blessing, the riches that you need for your calling will find you. That being said, how do you become a blessing? I'm so glad you asked.

To be a blessing, you must know about these inheritances, believe they belong to you, and receive them as yours. You can't *give* what you don't *have,* and you can't *have* what you don't *know.* John Courson explains it this way, "Blessings are like the measles -- you can't give 'em unless you got 'em!" [15] Ignorance is not bliss. It can cause you to miss out, but don't worry! You will easily understand these inheritances when they are given in detail later on. It's God's desire for you. Count on it.

God wanted the second born bride of Christ to inherit the firstborn material promised blessings of both the Old and the New Covenants, along with the spiritual blessings from heaven. God had prophetically showed this in the Old Testament through Abraham's seed, Isaac, then Isaac's descendant Jacob, and later through Jacob's sons, Judah and Joseph. Now it should continue to your seed through you.

In the New Testament, it was through Jesus, who was God's Son and Mary's baby, that the old inheritances could legally be connected with the New Covenant to include you. This brilliant plan made it possible to receive both the old and new promises that were needed to fulfill your destiny by divine design. God accomplished this phenomenal plan through Mary and Joseph. Would you like to know how?

CHAPTER 5 – THE LATTER CONNECTED TO THE FORMER

Although no one can go back and make a brand new start, anyone can start from now and make a brand new ending.

--Carl Bard

Why Were Mary and Joseph Chosen?

God needed a womb untainted by man for the birth of His Son. The virgin Mary was chosen, with her consent, and overshadowed by the Spirit to become pregnant with the seed of God--Christ, the Word. The Word received Mary's fleshly DNA and became a man to dwell among us as Jesus.

Chosen of God, think about this: when you were born again, you were honored to carry Christ's seed (His Spirit and DNA) in the womb of your spirit. Mary carried and birthed baby Jesus, but you get to conceive the Word of God in your heart and birth the truth and the promises of God. Similar to Mary, you flesh out the Word by seeing His promises come to pass on the earth. (see John 1:14)

Like Mary, your story was rewritten to bring you into your purpose--the reason for your birth. It began when you entered into a covenant marriage with Jesus. You became "pregnant" when you were overshadowed by the Holy Spirit. This made it possible for you to bring forth the promised possibilities and blessings from the spiritual realm into the physical world. These bridal inheritance promises, needed for your purpose, were to be accomplished by your faith in agreement with the Word, which is Jesus! It's not anything you did to merit this great honor. Jesus just can't stop blessing you, His bride and heir.

Of course, God loved Mary too, but I wondered why she was chosen for this honor? Only one person in the world could physically birth the Son of God, so why her? Have you ever thought on this? Obviously, she was highly favored by God, but was she better than all the other virgins who served God, or was she like us and had done nothing to merit this except to give her consent? Perhaps she wondered, "*Why me?*" And what did Joseph think? Was he included simply because he was engaged to Mary or was there another reason? He too must have questioned, "*Why us?*"

As I pondered this, I realized we couldn't know for certain, and maybe Mary was better than all the rest. However, through research, I came up with what I think to be a better answer. When I saw that Mary and Joseph were both from the royal Davidic line, bingo, the light came on. This was a huge clue and something massively mind-blowing. Because of these lineages, Christ could legally reign on David's throne, as prophesied, and this would result in you and me being extravagantly blessed!

Mary's ancestry was immensely important. Her lineage not only gave Jesus a lawful right to the throne of King David as a direct descendant, but also made it possible for all of us to inherit generational covenant blessings--don't miss this--retroactive all the way from Adam. *Oh, em, gee!*

Here's the proof. Mary's lineage began with Adam and went through King David and his son Nathan (see Luke 3). Here, Jesus was the Son of Adam (man) and Son of God (divinity) in her genealogy. Jesus Christ was both one hundred percent man and God equally, though He gave up his divine privileges; and He was born as a human being to die in proxy on the cross for you. (see Philippians 2:6-8, NLT) He was still God but chose to live in the restrictions of humanity.

Joseph's lineage in Matthew 1 began with Abraham and went through King David and his son, Solomon. Here, Jesus was called the Son of Abraham (faith/grace covenant) and Son of David (king). Jesus was equally High Priest of the grace covenant and King of God's kingdom.

Jesus, as the Son of Mary and Joseph (humanity) was called the Son of Adam (man), Son of Abraham (of the faith/grace covenant) and Son of David (king) for a reason. God made sure each one of these chosen forefathers had passed on the covenant blessings to the designated heir so the *material* blessings would come to Jesus and then to you, His covenant partner.

And because Christ was the Son of God through a virgin birth, His Father made sure the spiritual blessings would belong to you also. "Blessed be the God and Father of our Lord Jesus Christ, who has [past tense] blessed us with all spiritual blessings" (Ephesians 1:3, KJV). You have been given all of them! Both the physical and spiritual blessings are in your account for you to take hold of now!

The New (latter) had to be connected with the Old (former) for you to get the overflow of abundance needed for these last days. Wow! When you begin to see God's excessive unwarranted goodness towards you, favored one, it will take your breath away. God is crazy about you!

The Importance of the Virgin Birth

These wonderful *spiritual* inheritances in Revelation 5:12 of power, wealth, wisdom, might, honor, glory, and blessings obtained on the cross would not belong to you without a virgin birth. Did you know that? If Joseph was the biological father of Jesus, and God was not His Father, you would miss out on them. In other words, if you don't believe in the virgin birth, your inherited spiritual blessings would not belong to you. Yikes! This was so important that I began to wonder, could God have hidden more proof of this virgin birth, to remove all doubt? And yes, I found it!

There was more evidence concealed in Joseph's lineage. Joseph, Mary's husband, had an ancestor Jechonias, a descendant of Solomon. God said about Jechonias that no descendant of his would ever sit as king (see Jeremiah 22:30). This meant that if Jesus was the genetic son of Mary's husband, He could not be king, nor sit on the throne of David, or be the Messiah.

This verified that Jesus was not Joseph's son. He was adopted. There was no genetic tie or DNA link to Jechonias. Jesus was the King of kings and the Messiah. As the Son of God, He had God's spiritual DNA, and as the Son of Mary, he had her biological DNA. Joseph's genealogy was tainted, but not Mary's bloodline. It was clean. Beginning with Adam, the son of God, it continued through Abraham to David, from David to his son Nathan, from Nathan to Mary, and then to Jesus the *Son of Man*.

Jesus inherited the royal blood line as a genetic descendant with the DNA of King David and also the right to the priesthood through His mother's ancestry. He most likely inherited the throne of David also from Joseph's lineage, since He was adopted and not a biological descendant of Jechonias. It was evident; however, that God had made sure His Son was given indisputable legal rights to be the King of kings, sitting on David's throne, and the High Priest of priests forever!

All these meticulously detailed records of genealogies and posterities were kept for you, valued of God. Every jot and tittle was written so you could connect with your purpose and blessings. In addition, God made sure you arrived at the right time on earth to be born from the parents that carried the DNA needed that would make you – you, for your purpose. So obviously, your parents weren't by accident. They were carefully chosen by God. When I learned this, I was blown away.

My Descendants

I never expected what was about to happen when I reluctantly attended a family reunion. We had gone to the town cemetery to find the burial places of our ancestors. A relative had done research to discover that I came from a long bloodline of those who served God. That excited me and I grabbed those findings to wander away alone. Sitting on a tombstone, I began to read.

When I came to my great, great, great-grandfather I read that he was kept alive several times by what seemed to be the providence of God. When he was born, doctors said he would not live, but then it stated, "Yet, God revived him." Later, as a boy, he fell through the floor into the basement of an abandoned building and was there for three days with serious gashes and broken bones. Gangrene had set in, and he was not expected to live, but again, it read, "God revived him." I read story after story how God restored life back into his lifeless body seven or eight times.

Half-joking, I said to myself, "My goodness, his angels must have worked overtime to keep this dude alive!" My thoughts were abruptly interrupted when a voice rang out lovingly but fervently, "I had to keep him alive to get you here." What? Are you kidding me? How could that be? But then I saw what this meant. If he would have died any of those times I read about, before conceiving life, I would not be here, nor my mother and her ancestors.

I was wrecked and totally whacked at this revelation. God knew me before the foundation of the world. Angels must have been assigned to keep my ancestors alive long enough to pass on the seed that would eventually get me born into the lineage and dispensation planned by God. "He [God] chose us in Him before the foundation of the world" (Ephesians 1: 4, NKJV).

Was I that important and that valuable to God? It was a resounding *yes*! Before my birth, He thought about me to form my body in my mother's womb. Here's the proof: "I knew you before I formed you in your mother's womb. Before you were born I set you apart" (Jeremiah 1:5, NLT).

And David, a man after God's heart, knew about this as he wrote,

> You made all the delicate, inner parts of my body and knit me together in my mother's womb. Thank you for making me so wonderfully complex! You watched me as I was being formed in utter seclusion; as I was woven together in the dark of the womb. You saw me before I was born. Every day of my life was recorded in your book. Every moment was laid out before a single day had passed. How precious are your thoughts about me, O God. They cannot be numbered! I can't even count them; they out-number the grains of sand! And when I wake up you are still with me.
>
> --Psalm 139:13-18, NLT

Wow! Did you get this, loved of God? Really? You are extravagantly, passionately loved and wanted! And like my great grandfather, angels were assigned to watch over your ancestors and you because God planned your destiny before you were born. You were guarded by them, "For he shall give his angels charge over you to keep you in all your ways. They shall bear you up in their hands lest you dash your foot against a stone" (Psalm 91:11-12, AKJV).

This should mean more to you now, the magnificent covenant heritage you have been given with God, and added to this, your seed was also marked for the covenant! Oh, how tragic it must be for God when one of His babies is prevented from being birthed into the world. One aborted life is heart-breaking! An abortion doesn't affect just one baby, but an entire lineage. It causes the baby's future generations to be erased, literally. This is hard to fathom! God will always try to avert this unspeakable tragedy, but He will not violate a person's will.

Each child was planned by God. The Lord said, "See that you do not despise one of these little ones. For I tell you that their angels in heaven always see the face of my Father in heaven." (Matthew 18:10, NIV). They are His offspring and not a random happenstance. That is why all children go to heaven. They are greatly loved of Father God. Do you really understand the importance of your posterity as the bride of Christ and who you are to God?

God is the center of the Bible. Jesus is the hero of every story, but you are the cherished bride and His covenant partner. This makes you a joint heir of Jesus and an heir of God, staggeringly blessed and valued like Jesus Himself. Wow! Did you get this? You and your descendants are more precious to God than all of His creation, and your births were exuberantly celebrated in heaven. You are that important! That is why God gave you a covenant partnership with Jesus, so that you can find out why you were born and have a life the way it should be lived. Can anything be better than this? Doesn't this make you feel special?

CHAPTER 6 – BORN TO BE AN HEIR

To remember the other world in this world is to live in your true inheritance.

--David Whyte

You Were Born to Be Great!

The purpose for your birth should be more clear to you now, but I'll recap so you don't miss a thing. Drum roll, please! Jesus was born to answer the question for you and me, "Why was I ever born?" Jesus had to be born an heir of God and heir of man to get the birthrights and blessings from earth and heaven to pass on to you, His covenant partner and heir. Are you getting this yet?

The covenant is a partnership, with God and you together in every circumstance. You were born to be in a marriage covenant as one with Christ. Who He is, you are! "As He [Jesus] is, so also are we in this world!" (1 John 4:17b, CSB). As a *joint heir* you also inherit all He has and all He can do. (See John 16:14; 14:12.) "He [God] hath made Him to be sin for us, who knew no sin; that we might be made the righteousness of God in him" (2 Cor. 5:21, KJV). That makes you a purebred and eligible to receive it all. Woohoo! This is mind boggling! It's colossal! This should wipe out those pesky insecurities and timidities.

And there's more! Because of this marriage covenant with God's Son, you were born again into His family with new identities as children and heirs of His Father, God. Now don't forget this! You are a son and heir, never ever an orphan, alone, or abandoned. And you have inherited God's blessings and vast spiritual estate! (see Gal. 4:1) *Zowie!* Talk about an identity upgrade. This is huge!

As an important family member with the spiritual DNA of God your Father, you have all the divine blessings from heaven, plus the birthrights and blessings of Jesus's lineage from eons back. Beginning with Adam, it included the blessings of Abraham to Moses and on through King David. These were necessary for you to run God's kingdom business on earth, just like it is in heaven.

Oh yes! Did you know that you are Vice President of a Fortune 500-gazillion Company? You are a beneficiary of this kingdom as the second born in the family of God. "It is your Father's good pleasure to give you the kingdom" (Luke12:32, NKJV). As a kingdom citizen, you have position, protection, rights, resources, and power for the end time harvest. How awesome is that!

And because Jesus was legal heir to David's throne, you as the second born heir, have legal rights to co-reign on earth as kings and priests with Jesus Christ, the King of [us] kings and High Priest of [us] priests. It is by your kingly declarations and priestly prayers that you can cause God's kingdom to come into hard situations, changing it to be like heaven so that the will of God can be done on earth exactly like it is in heaven. Wow! This is beyond brilliant! (see Rev. 5:10; Matt. 6:10)

Everywhere you go on earth, Christ's Kingdom and His Spirit is in you and in charge. Everything you want to *be, have* or *do* lies within, through the new man--the inner man of the spirit that communicates with Holy Spirit. And concurrently, because you are *in covenant*, your spirit is *in Christ*, seated in heavenly places in the presence of God with dominion over the things of the earth. And this, blessed one, is a gigantic "*neener-neener*" to the devil. He can't win with Jesus as your co-partner!

Your kingdom citizenship is in heaven with access to legalities of the King's standards, precepts, and laws of justice and righteousness. This is what God calls right, the way it should be. In addition, on earth, you have the position of kingdom ambassador, representing God and your heavenly home country to others while introducing them to God. Did you get this? Heaven invades earth through you! You were born to bring heaven to earth until the Lord's return.

God meant for you to live under the blessed jurisdiction of the governmental Kingdom of God and to not have to depend on the cursed systems of this world. God is your Source and your only source! "Seek the kingdom of God above all else and he will give you everything you need" (Luke 12:31, NLT). You need these covenant blessings to fulfill your destiny, as well as to have outrageous influence on the earth and to show the goodness of God while doing the kingdom works of Abraham, David, and Jesus. If Satan had known about these plans for you, he wouldn't have plotted to kill the King of Glory.

Obstacles Precede Covenant Inheritances

You are now the devil's worst enemy. Demonic forces are opposed to you getting your inheritances and the fulfillment of your destiny, because when you get them, they know it will be their demise. So, evil will try to keep you confused by bringing trials, deceptions, distractions, delays, pain, or offenses. Even life itself has resistances and contradictions that can try to undermine your purpose, which was pre-written in Heaven's books before you were born.

I bet you can relate. Have you been bombarded by resistances and, because of it, you're confused and struggling to keep the faith? Have hard situations veiled your vision or the voice of

God? Has fear or doubt distorted your perception, and you see no way out? Well, I understand those battles. I've been there and done that. Just like you, I face these same kinds of challenges. We are all in this together, but I want more of God for you and me. And God wants us winning in life, blessed to be a blessing. By going through opposition, we receive the preparations to succeed in our destinies.

So fear not, courageous one! Think on this! "Breakthrough and promotion are on the other side of obstacles and opposition," says Bill Johnson. [16] Trials are meant to bring joy. In other words, hardships are the steppingstones to upgrades and the prerequisites for greatness. Every problem has a promise for a solution that will bring lavish provision when discovered. That's right. Treasures are hidden in the darkness with secret riches to possess that makes it all worthwhile. (see Isaiah 45:3)

Jeff Wittmer says, "The enemy fears that the fire he sent to destroy you, will instead be used to ignite the power and potential within you." [17] Yes, that is so true! Challenges are meant to unlock your potential and give you unexpected opportunities to become more like Christ, as well as to have successful outcomes and overcome every presented obstacle. So go for the gold! Get God's best.

Learning how to use the promises and respond wisely and responsibly to worldly difficulties are very important parts of your story. Even Jesus had to go through these kinds of hardships when He chose to come to earth as a baby and be exposed to offenses, curses, and the negative programming by the devil. He also faced imperfect parents, jealous siblings, and difficult relationships. (see Hebrews 5:8)

It was necessary for Him to learn as a human how to defeat Satan by using God's word. Jesus would say, "It is written," to overcome His carnal appetites, the devil, and the influences of a depraved, cursed world that negatively affected thinking and believing (see Matthew 4:4). God could not ask you to overcome what His Son had not. Of course, Jesus did overcome all opposition: "Be of good cheer I have overcome the world" (John 16:33b, KJV). Now God's promises will cause you to overcome too. You have the power through His word to become like Christ and win every time!

God's GPS System

The magnificent covenant blood is the source of that power. Even if you get off course or stuck on your journey, God will remember His covenant (see Psalm 105:8). God's Positioning System (His GPS) will *recalibrate* your life to reestablish His identity of you as an overcoming heir and bring you back into your bountiful predestined inheritances. Isaiah 30:21 (NLT) says, "Your own ears will hear Him. Right behind you, a voice will say… ['Recalculating.']" The verse continues, saying, "This is the way you should go, whether to the right or to the left." Ha! Did you see that you're made unstoppable and unbeatable!

Obviously, there will be problems and difficult people that will try to mess you up. (Ya think?) But when you discover *who God is for you* (who He wants to be for you in each situation) and *who God says you are* (your true identity), you will overcome any hardship. The purpose of *why you were born* (your corporate purpose) was about being a joint heir with Jesus, an heir of God and an heir of Abraham. Being an heir enabled you to receive the birthrights and blessings allotted to you that will be needed for what you are called to do, *why you are here now* (your personal destiny). (See Revelation 21:7) Being blessed is in your spiritual DNA. It's part of your destiny!

Bill Winston in *Commanding the Blessing* says,

> The blessing guarantees your success. It will take you to the top. The blessing brings stuff to you. It brings

> ideas and opportunities; it brings resources. Adam was made like God and that's why the animals were brought to him. The blessing gave Adam and Eve the choice of empowerment and enablement to fulfill their assignment without toil or struggle. [18]

Proverbs 10:22 (NIV) confirms this, "The blessing of the Lord brings wealth without painful toil for it." Sadly, Adam and Eve didn't believe God and, being cast out of the garden, struggled.

You were not born to be a victim in bondage and under the elements of this world! No, over-coming one, instead you were meant to be under the covenant blood to dominate and make a difference in this world! But like Adam and Eve, it's your choice. They chose to disobey God, which brought them great struggle.

Let this not be said of you! You were made to live in the blessings of the Lord and to believe His word and prosper. The Blessing will make you an overcomer! You were born to overcome difficult situations and circumstances so you can rule over the devil and reign on the earth. Your story matters! So, isn't it time to let your story be re-written to His Story?

CHAPTER 7 – FOOLISH CHOICES

But God chose the foolish things of the world to shame the wise; God chose the weak things of the world to shame the strong.

--1 Corinthians 1:27, NIV

Sinner or Saint?

Maybe you don't feel victorious. Perhaps it's because when life's experiences messed you up, you made some foolish choices and let those mess ups define who you are. That's what I did too, but it is not just about you or me or what we did. It's about God and the sum total of situations, experiences, and people. This being so, why would you blame yourself to be ridden with guilt and shame or accuse others?

Take a look at John 8:7 (BSB), which says, "Let him who is without sin among you be the first to cast a stone at her." Oops! Not one of us can accuse another innocently. I think this means that we are supposed to put our stones down. What do you think? Even those in the Bible messed up. Noah got drunk, Abraham lied, Jacob deceived, Moses murdered, Rahab was a prostitute, David had an affair, Sampson lusted, Gideon was a coward, the Samaritan woman had five husbands, Mary Magdalene had seven demons, Paul was a serial killer, and Peter denied Christ. Yet God was able to bless and use them all.

So now what excuse can we use to judge anyone, including ourselves? I admit it, my foolish choices were probably more embarrassing than yours, but the good news is that God does not *behold* our mistakes, big or small, nor does He condemn anyone. He knows about our ugly mess ups, and we are held responsible to deal with them. However, God's focus is not on sin but on the potential to reveal our purpose.

A good example of this is in the Old Testament where the prophet Balaam was sent by an enemy king to curse Israel. Even though Israel had frequently sinned against God during their journey in the wilderness, the prophet could not curse them. They were in covenant with God, and whoever God blessed could not be cursed. But then I read something that really confused me. It said, "He, [God] hath not *beheld* iniquity in Jacob, neither hath he seen perverseness in Israel" (Numbers 23:21, KJV).

My initial thought was, "Are you kidding me?" I certainly could see a whole lot of sin and rebellion in their camps. Why couldn't God? Was He not telling the truth about them? Then I saw it. God was aware of their iniquities, and the people experienced consequences because of them, but that was not His focus.

God was not *beholding* their wrongs. His attention was on their purpose and destiny. He spoke into their potential, how He saw them, and who they really were, so that they could become it. God saw the oak tree (the invisible truth) in the acorn and had a plan to fulfill why they were born. Oh God! Help us see the truth, the spiritual reality of who we really are! Let truth expose every lie. Let love undo every agenda.

Restored Destiny

Here is a good example of God bringing out potential: in the New Testament, the Samaritan woman at the well had also made foolish choices, six that we know of. The result was five failed marriages and settling for living with a man. Her need for love had gone unmet. Broken and looking for love in all the wrong places, she was stuck in her story like I once was. Oh how I get this! She must have wondered, "Why was I ever born?" (see John 4)

Unable to escape her cyclic lifestyle, she had settled for less than who she was meant to be. Jesus was the only one who could restore her to the destiny she really wanted to live. He knew about her mess ups and spoke about them to her, but without judgment. He was not disappointed in her. Jesus just wanted to show others who He saw her to be. Now, she could be respected for who she really was and not tried and condemned for those foolish choices made during life's hardships.

Without reproving her, Jesus called her up to a greater destiny and a more fulfilling life of impacting an entire city. It was from this vantage point of His love and acceptance that she could begin to see herself as He saw her and start making better choices. One encounter with Jesus and her life was changed dramatically. She could now begin to live a story written for her by God.

Casting aside the shame of her dirty laundry, she no longer avoided the people of her city who had judged her. Instead, she ran to tell them about a man that had known about all of her mistakes, yet loved her anyway. Her passion was undeniable, and her hope was catching. It was apparent something was very different about her. The change was drastic. Where did this confidence and fearlessness come from? They had to know, and when they found Jesus, their lives drastically changed too.

Her name was not revealed, and I think this was to protect her. We tend to remember the negative more than the positive. Don't we? If someone mentioned her name, wouldn't we say, "Oh yeah, she is the one who had five husbands?" Shouldn't we say, "Oh yes, she is the one who saved her city." Admit it, we usually remember others by past mistakes instead of how far they have come. The truth is that we all have erred and come short of God's glory (See Romans 3:23). Brian Simmons, writer of the Passion Bible, concurs, "Every one of us has been married to our five husbands; our five senses. Christ is our real husband; the only One who satisfies."[19]

It is easy to forget we all have made foolish choices at times when swayed by emotions or hurtful situations. Even so, I don't want to give the impression that I'm making excuses for sin and poor choices or emphasizing the injustice of wrongs done to us, because I am not. These have consequences. But the point I want to make is that God wants to deal with our mess ups and heal our wounds, and He does it through a process that will help us make good and right choices.

Your journey is meant to bring out hidden potential and the discovery of who you really are in Christ. And even if you have messed up or been wronged, your background doesn't matter! Life is not about the past or even the happy ending. You're not defined by a chapter, but by your story. That's why I love the story of the Samaritan woman. It's my story too. Can you relate?

The Tapestry called Life

I had a pattern of foolish choices with three marriage mistakes before encountering Jesus. Yet God wove the darkness of my past into a tapestry that told my story, and He used all of it to make me who I am today. At times I could only see jumbled threads and dark colors on the back side, and nothing seemed to make sense. Then God showed me that this was only a dark chapter, not the whole book! He began to add bright hues of colors and patterns that stood out from the black.

When He turned the tapestry over to give me a glimpse of who He had made me to be, I could see it was the dark threads that made the vibrant colors pop with astonishing beauty. God had wasted nothing in my life, bad or good, but included it all.

He weaved everything together for the good by rewriting my story so I could see my beauty. He even answered my question, "Why was I born?"

I really wanted to live life to the fullest, to come alive and know why I was here on this planet. My passion for a good and meaningful life was not a negative craving. It was God given.

Aren't you desirous of a life that counts? Perhaps you are caught up in the "rat race" and want out. Maybe you are wondering why you were born and why you are here, like I used to wonder.

Do you think your birth is only a byproduct of your parents "romp in the hay," and you just happened to arrive nine months later? Can there be a reason for your birth--a calling, purpose, or destiny by divine design? Who are you, really? And what are you meant to be and do? Between your birth-date and death-date, will these questions have been answered and lived out in your life, or will you die without having delivered why you were put on this earth?

Part of your purpose is to be a good influence to your family. Yes indeed, but it's also about impacting the lives of others. So will you let these undelivered talents and dreams lay some-day buried in a grave while others miss out on what you had and what they needed? Well take courage, it's not over. It's not the end.

Unregretted Risks and Pursued Dreams

You don't have to regret the risks you didn't take or the dreams you didn't pursue--you know, those dreams that chose you and won't let go. You were built to live out these kinds of dreams in an allotted time. Right now you have been given time to begin again and change your future. So stop wasting valuable time! There will be no do-overs in the sweet by and by. Get rid of the *que sera sera* attitude--"whatever will be, will be." No, it won't!

You determine your future right now, today!

Of course, it will not always be easy. There will be obstacles to overcome and hardships along the way. And yes, it can be difficult or painful at times, but you can either experience the pain of regret or suffer pain on the road of discovering the real you. Opposition is meant to help you think with a new perspective which is much bigger and better. Satan sends resistance trying to destroy you, but God uses it to set you free from the world, yourself, and the devil.

The choice is yours. No one can keep you from your destiny, but you! Co-create your future with God. He will always bring you into your destiny that was written in the covenant blood of Jesus and perhaps even written in your genetic code. Did you know that some rabbis believe that God put a memory in your DNA of what you're destined to become, and everything God does has already been recorded?

God wants to eradicate regret and develop in you the power to endure. You can hold on when things go wrong, face defeat without giving up, and be unstoppable and relentless against opposition. These are winner's qualities. So courageous one, go the distance! Keep going! Never give up!

Graham Cooke says, "Every negative situation has a job to do in your life. Your current circumstances are ideal soil for your next breakthrough in Christ. You will not get a better opportunity than right now to become brilliant, to take a step up into a higher place of favor and promise."[20]

A changed future starts with changed thinking. Maybe you need a revolution of your identity like I did, a change in the way you think or see yourself. And yep, it's usually easier to change external things like spouses, jobs, houses and friends, but guess what? If the inner man isn't changed, you will remain the same person and not become who you really are--who God created you to be.

Kathi Pelton agrees, "If you are living under an identity that is short of amazing beauty, then you are not living in God's image or His design for your life." [21] Oh yes! Take time to know God and your true identity so that you can win your races. If you're *in Christ,* you can't lose. Since God is with you, He always wins. It's a done deal! There are victory prizes laid up for you and blessings galore with your name on them that are yours for the taking. Victorious one, run to win! "Run in such a way as to win the prize" (1 Corinthians 9:24, CSB). God will deliver you from anything that might hinder you, such as fear, insecurity, despair, or bitterness.

You can't lose if you don't quit. Destinies are waiting to be fulfilled because you've been called to be significant and outstanding! Of course, no one feels prepared or qualified to win. Run anyway, confident that when you trust God and believe in His goodness, the victories are yours in every situation you face. Then you can say, "I have fought the good fight, I have finished the race, I have kept the faith" (2 Tim. 4:7, NKJV). So, I ask you, do you believe it? Are you willing to go the distance and win? If so, *"Get ready! Get set! Go discover!*

CHAPTER 8 – FROM VICTIM TO OVERCOMER

We need to be careful not to fall into the victim mindset. This usually happens because we have a disempowering perspective of the circumstance. We forget about "who we are" in Christ.

--Michael Barbarulo

Who Do I Think I Am?

The Lord had to rewrite my story and take me from a victim identity to that of an overcomer, because I really didn't know who I was. Prior to Christ, I had chosen men like my father--handsome womanizers. After becoming a Christian, I actually thought that I was making the right choice when I married, but *oy vey*, I had messed up again! This time I married someone with traits not necessarily like my father's, but more like my mother's: critical, neglectful, and emotionally unavailable. There were parts of me still broken. I was undeveloped in certain areas, and my "chooser" was deficient too. My identity was still that of a junk mare, living my life by chance as a victim of circumstance instead of living with intention, by God's design.

Even as a Christian, I was pathetically needy, so much so that my needs dictated my life. Have you ever been there? Everything was about me. At first, I tried to get God to change my husband so my needs could be met; after all, wasn't he the problem? Yes, he was part of it, but so was I! I had a weak identity. It was not a makeover or a behavior modification that I needed, but to realize who God says I am, then, live by that identity as a new creation.

I knew this marriage was *not* made in heaven. We were both broken, but I finally realized my life would not get better by chance, only by change. For real change to happen, I had to change; so, I stopped blaming my husband to let God heal and develop me. As I submitted to God, He did that and so much more! He made me unrecognizable to who I once was and brought lasting change in me. It wasn't that He fixed me. He actually killed my deficient "old man" to make me totally new with a new heart and mind of Christ. He gave me a fresh new life made in heaven.

The Heavenly Life

God changed my life drastically and brought me into an intimate partnership with Him that I did not know was possible. He began showing me that people, circumstances, or situations should not dictate my life anymore. Did you know this? I sure didn't, but as I learned about it, this marriage became one of the best things that ever happened to me. Why so? Because in it, I was changed!

God set me free from the captivity of others wrongs and even my own negative cyclical patterns. The over and over was over. I no longer was dependent on another's behavior or treatment of me. What mattered was how I showed up in love and confidence. God turned my pitiful expressions of needy love into unconditional love, as well as changed my "stinkin-thinkin'" into expectant believing.

When I found out *who God was for me* personally, He became my Hero, my everything. By discovering how good God was as my Father and how gigantically generous Jesus was as my Covenant partner, I found *who I really am in Christ*, just because He says I am. Holy Spirit began showing me glimpses of what my heavenly Father thinks of me and *who I am to God.*

And guess what? God thinks I am His hero. Think on that! Now that will blow your mind and play with your inadequacies! I am the center of His world and valued beyond the creation. Oh yeah! That's because He wanted me to see as He does, so that my story could be rewritten. "God rewrote the text of my life when I opened the book of my heart to his eyes" (Psalms 18:24, MSG).

Loved one, you may not know it yet, but this is your story too! You have to be willing to see it in His word and believe it, or this great truth will pass you by. Why not ask God to show you what He thinks of you even in the midst of screw ups? The discoveries will be endless and humbly intoxicating.

The pages of my life book began turning as God wrote new chapters in them. When I discovered things that belonged to me as a *co-heir* with Jesus, I became the recipient of amazing blessings. For the first time, I was winning and no longer stuck in my story. I went from a gloomy life to a glorious one, from a victim to an overcomer; I was delivered, loved, and greatly blessed of God.

My story was rewritten so I would no longer believe I was junk, a mistake, or behave like a cat that chases her tail. That was who I used to be. I now live like the cat that constantly lands on her feet. When I stand on the word, I always win in the end with a successful outcome that is God's will. God delivers me out of every trial because I'm learning the "who" and the "why." *Who* God is for me (His identity) and *who* I am to God (my identity); *why* I was born (heir of blessings) and *why* I am here now (personal destiny and assignments).

I Was a Sinner, but Now *I Am* a Saint

I am a new creation, born anew, and new babies have no past. There are still days that I wish some things that happened in the past could be changed, but I can't go back or alter them.

And guess what? In God's eyes, they never existed. In this covenant with Christ, I was forgiven; thus, all my sins (past-present-future) were buried with Jesus. It's not who I am today. I am no longer a sinner saved by grace. That label of sinner was who *I was* until saved by God's glorious grace.

Now *I am* the righteousness of God, even though I may occasionally sin (see 2 Cor. 5:17-21). His righteousness defines me, not my behavior. God loves me, not because I am good, but because He is good. My life is not about looking back but moving forward in His covenant love and blessing. The rear-view mirror of my car is so much smaller compared to the size of my windshield, reminding me that where I am headed is much more important than what I've left behind.

I used to hide my past in embarrassment and fear of being judged or rejected. But no longer! My life is totally transformed and visibly different. My history of who *"I was"* doesn't matter. The "old man" as a poor, devalued, victimized nurse mare's foal was buried with Jesus in the grave and ceased to exist (something I desperately wanted as a teen). Jesus's cross was for the burial of that old sinner, the wimpy, wussy, whiner identity. The junk "old man" passed away. She's dead. R.I.P.!

Then, in the resurrection, I was raised up with Jesus as an entirely new creation. That is why I refuse to live like the walking dead by robbing the grave and digging up the past of who I used to be. Zombies aren't the way to live, the resurrection glory is! So don't judge me by my past, because I don't live there anymore. I live in the *New* Covenant of the Risen Christ that changed who *I am*.

You see, when Jesus was crucified, God saw me *in Him*. He hung there, not *for me* but *as me*. When He was buried, all the sin of my "old man" was left in the grave. As He was raised from the dead, I was raised to a new life as a "new man." Then, when He ascended to be glorified and seated on high, I also was raised and seated with Him in position, nobility, and power--thus, having legal access to heavenly realms of glory.

When God looks at me, He sees me through His Son. As Christ is, *I am* to God. I now live from another realm and think from a higher perspective through the new man. I can see things from God's perspective. It was this amazing covenant blood that transformed me from "*I was*" to "*I am,*" living in the power of the resurrection. It's who "*I am*" that counts.

To God, *I am* always good enough just as *I am*, though His goodness keeps making me better. God defined me and made me beautiful by clothing me with His glory. And yes, *I am* a trophy wife again, but this time, a trophy of His grace and covenant love. *I am* a masterpiece of God's imagination. *I am* His accomplishment! God loves to make junk mare foals into Triple Crown winners by replacing the old mindsets with new ones; to think like champions. And this folks happens to be a shameless, illogical, brazen, bodacious change from that of my childhood!

So let's stop judging people's pasts and instead see people through the blood. Someone once said, "Before you judge my life, my past or my character, walk in my shoes; walk the path I have traveled, live my sorrow, my doubts, my fear, my pain and my laughter. . . Remember that everyone has a story. When you've lived my life, then you can judge me." [22] Now that, my friend, is wisdom! (Unknown source)

It was Christ's blood covenant that put me in His bloodline with His DNA and changed my story. *I am* actually a neon sign of what God can do with brokenness and failure when there is true repentance. Kris Valloton agrees:

> God loves to show the world what He can do through you. He can turn a five times divorcee into a marriage counselor. He uses those who have failed, to build those

> who are ruined. Jesus is a master of making palaces out of pitfalls. It does not matter how far you have fallen or how big a mess you've made out of your life. God is the God of impossibilities. [23]

Oh yeah! That is so right.

God loves to take mess ups and make them into His messages. He loves you too much to let you stay messy, insignificant, or irrelevant. Your past and who you once were as a sinner is to be forever buried. Rise up from "I was" to "I am." God wants to rewrite your story. He is calling you right now. Will the "new you" (not the "I was" you), the "true you" (the "I am" you), the "blessed you," please stand up!

CHAPTER 9 – YOUR LIFE STORY REWRITTEN

Life isn't about finding yourself; it's about discovering who God created you to be.

--Author Unknown

Day of Discovery: Who do You Think You Are?

Daring one, you too can have destinies beyond your wildest dreams, but that depends on what you believe about yourself. But no worry! God will rewrite your story and wake you up to who you really are! It's a life changer when you discover the person you already are *in Christ* (in covenant) and learn to behave accordingly. God is crazy, over-the-moon in love with you. In your story, you are His beloved bride, because your story has been intercepted by His Story.

The covenant blood of the cross and the power of the resurrection have changed everything. Now, when you repent, even your failures have a purpose and need not define your destiny. They can become feedback--your present wisdom, as God directs and details why you were born. So, child of destiny, why don't you stop letting your humanity disappoint you and begin to live who you really are to God?

God's purpose for you is so much bigger than you realize. What is your story? Are you dangerous to the enemy because of your story or are you living as a poor nurse mare's foal, beneath who God says you are, like I once did? Are you in bondage to what others have put on you? Have you been a prisoner of their wrongs and rejections, or your own negative patterns that you can't break? Did you ever fight loneliness or make poor decisions that kept you from fulfilling your dreams?

"Some of you have been in your situation for so long, it's become your identity," says Jennifer Eivaz. "The Word of God is your identity! It's time to get a new word about that situation." [24] Yes, your story is to be about living the life God designed for you. You're meant to win in life. Your story will become bigger than you when you understand covenant love with God and the inheritances that belong to you (those not earned by your behavior, but by the cross). (For further insight, go to my website, thelostcovenant.com, for short videos about covenant and what exchanges were accomplished on the cross that are your inheritances.)

As you continue, you will be able to take ownership of these covenant inheritances that will cause you to win in difficult situations. However, if you don't claim the upgrades of the birthrights, blessings, and benefits, you will live beneath your privileges. God wants none of these benefits to be left in your heavenly account. All are meant for use down here on the earth (See 1 Peter 1:3).

King David knew this and admonished covenant keepers to not forget all the benefits of God's covenants (See Psalms 103:2, 18). And Ezra wrote, "Remember his covenant forever, The word which He commanded, for a thousand generations, The covenant which He made with Abraham, And His oath to Isaac, And confirmed it to Jacob for a statute, To Israel for an everlasting covenant." (1Chron. 16:15-17, NKJV).

The Lost Covenant of the Kingdom

Jesus had taken the curse to reconnect you to all the covenant blessings that you were meant to inherit. Do you know what these blessings are? And if so, have you remembered the benefits and received them as your own? Oops, somehow, they have been forgotten, or overlooked, haven't they? I think the new covenant took a back seat to the kingdom of God and became almost lost to all of us. Perhaps we thought it insignificant or less exciting than the kingdom with its power, signs, and wonders.

Could this be why we struggle to know who we really are in Christ through the covenant? Perhaps when we join both the kingdom and covenant together in these last days, the whole house of God will be represented in its fullness. "The glory of the latter house shall be greater than the former, saith the Lord of Hosts" (Haggai 2:9, KJV).

The kingdom and covenant are near kinsmen; blood relatives and are equally important. Perhaps, they can be compared to fraternal twins; distinctive but not identical. They are similar to Judah's congenital twins; Zerah and Pherez. Zerah made his appearance on the earth as the first born twin. He represented the kingdom. Designated as the first born, Zerah later drew back and Pherez, the second to appear, received the firstborn birthrights and blessings. Pherez represented the covenant. Could this be prophetic of the kingdom and covenant that Jesus would bring?

Jesus brought and demonstrated the kingdom first (like Zerah). He began his ministry saying, "Repent for the kingdom of heaven is at hand" (Matthew 4:17 ESV). He taught the kingdom throughout His ministry until the Last Supper when His focus changed to the new covenant. It was at that time that the kingdom, (like Zerah) drew back. The New Covenant (like Pherez) made it possible for the firstborn birthrights and blessings of Jesus to go to the second born heir. Jesus' words just prior to the cross were, "This cup [of blessing] is the new covenant in my blood, which is poured out for you." (Luke 22:20 NIV)

Can you see it? The covenant and kingdom go together! Jesus

said, "Very truly I tell you, no one can see the kingdom of God unless they are born again." (John 3;3 NIV) The inherited covenant blessings enabled the second born heirs to advance the kingdom in its full perception.

The Kingdom First

Jesus had proclaimed and demonstrated the kingdom first, before He taught that salvation comes by being born again through a covenant with Christ. Did you know that, inquiring one? I thought salvation was to be presented first, didn't you? Now I was curious. I had to find out, so I began to research this puzzling order. Perhaps a clue to it was in what Jesus said in Luke 16:16 (NLT): "The Good News of the Kingdom of God is preached, and everyone is eager to get in."

Jesus was saying that the kingdom will be so exciting, and it will have the attention of all people because of its good news. Jesus told His disciples, "Go and announce to them that the Kingdom of Heaven is near. Heal the sick, raise the dead, cure those with leprosy, and cast out demons" (Matt 10:7-8, NLT). Did you notice that He didn't say, "Go and tell them they are sinners in need of salvation"?

It was the supernatural displays that attracted multitudes. John 2:23b (KJB) says, "Many believed in his name when they saw the miracles which he did." Why was this so? Well, wouldn't you want to be healed or delivered or have your lack multiplied to surplus? Aren't you desirous of getting your problems solved and to experience something far greater than yourself? Isn't this more appealing than, "Get saved or burn in hell"? Even so, some might need to be snatched from the fire through fear. Ha! (See Jude 1:23, KJV).

After witnessing these demonstrations of the kingdom, Nicodemus, a Pharisee, was so captivated by it that he sought Jesus late at night. He was very eager to be a part of it, but Jesus instead offered him the covenant, "Very truly I tell you, no one can see the kingdom of God unless they are born again" (John 3:3, NIV). It was the kingdom with its power and culture of love that made the covenant of salvation so desirable. Perhaps this kingdom was presented first so that people could know they need a Savior who loves them and is very present to help them.

The Kingdom – The Power Acts of God; What God Does

The kingdom is about the powerful *acts* of God (miracles, signs, and wonders) – it is what God *does*. Now think on this. This kingdom you've been given to bring God's will to earth, comes with much tribulation and violent opposition; thus, you must be forceful, strong, and courageous. It isn't going to be easy peasy, folks "The kingdom of heaven suffers violence and violent men take it by force" (Matt.11:12, NASB) .

John Eldredge contrasts the kingdom like this: "The kingdom of heaven is open to passive, wimpy men who enter it by living on the couch watching TV. If you are going to live in God's kingdom, Jesus says, it's going to take every ounce of passion and forcefulness you've got. Things are going to get fierce, that's why you were given a fierce heart." [25]

Since that is the case, mighty warrior, I ask you, how can you *fully* advance God's kingdom by force if you're ignorant of your covenant identity, inheritance rights and resources? Obviously, you can't. To serve Christ in His kingdom power, you must seek to live uprightly in integrity, thoughts and deeds of the Holy Spirit; receive His peace in midst of storms and the joy of the Lord as your strength. (See Romans 14:17, 18 NKJV) Also, it is essential that you use what has been allotted to you through His covenant.

Covenant – Intimacy with God; the Ways of God

Covenant is about *intimacy* with God; being one with Christ and partnering with God's will and plans. It is the *ways* of God— God's ways reveal His character, who He is, how He thinks, and who He made you to be. Your identity is revealed in covenant. This marriage covenant comes with inherited benefits and blessings because you are His beloved bride. When you are *"in Christ"* it means *"in covenant."* As God is, so are you! And all that He has, you have, and the works God did while on earth and greater works, you can do. Zowie! This is your identity!

Covenant is that pathway to a life of the miraculous. It is *"the cup of Blessing"* and *"the constitution"* of God's governmental kingdom that gives heaven legal right to come to earth and make your life extraordinary. This is the time for the kingdom and covenant to come together. Can you see that each is significant, like the wings of a plane? Ask the pilot which one is most important. I think you get the point.

The kingdom was intentionally connected to the New Covenant: "But seek first the Kingdom of God and his righteousness, and all these things will be added to you" (Matthew 6:33, ESV). Everything and every issue in life had been reduced to first seeking both the kingdom of God (power) and His righteousness (right standing with God, by being born again in covenant). Then, when both the kingdom and covenant are joined together, everything you have need of for your calling will find you.

This is the season to renew this amazing covenant and to make it the center of your life. So, buckle your seat belt, buckaroo! God is about to rewrite your story so that you might be really good at being you. Revelation is about to be unlocked and blessings uncovered that will unrelentingly run you down and knock you over. It's time for you to be blissfully whacked by His blessings!

CHAPTER 10 – A PRICELESS TREASURE WAITING TO BE DISCOVERED

Seek, and ye shall find.

--Matthew 7:7b, KJV

Discover the Treasures of the New Covenant

It is the appointed time to discover the treasures of the New Covenant. David Wilkerson, a great prophetic voice, understood the new covenant to be a mystery that had been hidden for years and was the secret to waking up the last day church. He kept seeking diligently for revelation of the New Covenant since the age of twenty-five and was privileged to begin seeing it forty plus years later. He alleged that the covenant was assigned to the end time's dispensation, which would meet all our needs, and when connected with the kingdom would enable us to fully unleash the power to advance God's kingdom.[26]

Could this be a mystery to be revealed at the right season? Paul speaks about mysteries: "The mystery which has been hidden from ages and from generations, but now has been revealed to His saints" (Colossians 1:26; Ephesian 3:4-6 NKJV). We see in Galatians 3:23 that faith was shut up to those under the law until it was revealed in the dispensation of the New Covenant. God reveals secrets at the proper time like the seashore whose sands recede with the tide, exposing the hidden treasure. Treasures are meant to be discovered by those attuned and seeking after them. Ignorance is not bliss, folks. It can cause you to miss out. Here's a true story that exemplifies what ignorance can do.

The Joshua Bell Story

A man stood at a Metro station in Washington DC playing the violin; it was a cold January morning. He played Bach, Brahms, and Schubert pieces--no pop tunes of familiarity, but masterpieces that have endeared for centuries. Three minutes went by when a middle-aged man noticed there was a musician playing. He slowed his pace and stopped for a few seconds, then hurried along. A minute later, the violinist received his first dollar tip; a woman threw the money in the till as she walked by. A few minutes later someone leaned against the wall to listen to him, but the man looked at his watch and started to walk again. A shoeshine attendant almost called the police because he was offended by the noise of the violin that interfered with his business.

The man played for about forty-five minutes. During that time, it was calculated that thousands of people from every culture passed by, not even turning their heads in that direction. Even those standing at the kiosks to buy something paid no attention. It seemed as though he was invisible. Perhaps to some it was deliberate inattention, so they didn't feel guilty about not forking over any money.

The one who paid the most attention was a three-year-old boy. His mother hurried him along as the child stopped to look. Finally, the mother pushed hard to drag him off as he kept looking back towards the sound of the beautiful music. This action was repeated by several other children. All the parents, without exception, forced them to move on. Only six people stopped for a minute. Twenty people gave him money but continued to walk. He collected a paltry thirty-two dollars. When he finished playing and silence took over, no one noticed. No one applauded. No crowd had gathered, nor was there any recognition except from one woman who planted herself front and center.

None of the people knew that this violinist was Joshua Bell, a Jewish child prodigy and internationally acclaimed virtuoso who played to standing room only, where the cheap seats were over $100 and his talent often commanded upwards of $1,000 *per minute*. He had just played some of the most intricate pieces of music ever written. His Stradivarius violin was worth over $3.5 million dollars.

Joshua Bell playing incognito in the metro station was organized by the Washington Post as part of a social experiment about perception, taste, and priorities of people. It was a commonplace environment at an inappropriate hour. This was an experiment to see if beauty would transcend--if people were *capable* of recognizing this treasure in a chaotic environment, or if people simply don't care anymore.

It was derived that one of the possible conclusions from this experience could be if we didn't have a moment to stop and listen to one of the best musicians in the world playing the finest music ever written, how many other things were we missing? This was thought provoking, for sure.

Child of blessing, are we like the subway people who missed a treasure, hidden in plain sight? This is a story of hidden riches in secret places, treasures placed around us waiting to be discovered. (See Isaiah 45:3) The unnoticed Stradivarius is a perfect example of the *new covenant*; it is an untapped treasure and priceless gift to mankind that is being revealed now in this dispensation. The sound from the violin is like the sound of heaven, the *kingdom of God* coming to earth. And Joshua Bell, the master musician who sacrificed his life and time to release this treasure to the world, points us to Jesus, our Master. Jesus paid His very life to give us the inherited riches, benefits, and blessings of both the new covenant and the kingdom of God. How in the world have we missed these treasures hidden, not from us, but for us?

The Parable of the Sower (Mark 4)

The Lord told us how to obtain the treasures of the kingdom but warned against the things that would cause us to miss out. He said Satan stole the word of the kingdom from the people because they were ignorant or complacent. (This was like the thousands that passed by Joshua Bell unaware of the blessings.) Jesus also spoke of stony hearts where some get immediately offended with the message (very much like the shoeshine attendant who thought the noise of the violin interfered with business as usual). Then there were those who let the cares of this world choke out the blessing (like the busy man who looked at his watch and left). And it was the deceitfulness of riches that made others miss out on the true treasure (like those who paid no attention while standing by the kiosks to buy something).

Few found the treasure. "Narrow is the gate which leads to life and there are few who find it" (Matthew 7:14, NKJV). The woman who planted herself front and center and the young children who had to be dragged away were the only ones that found the treasure. They were like those with a good heart who hear, see, and receive the beauty, blessings, and benefits of this great treasure.

Perhaps this has more meaning to you now, "Unless you turn around and become like little children, you will never enter the kingdom of heaven" (Matthew 18:3, NET). Maybe we need to grow up and become childlike. Little children are instinctively drawn to the sounds of heaven. Born with the innate knowledge of another realm, children are spiritually discerning and always exploring to discover new things.

It's time to play hide and seek, child of God, to search after what has been hidden for you to discover. You are about to find hidden riches in secret places. Concealed within the new covenant of the kingdom are ancient treasures of old. The new covenant intentionally pointed to the old covenant of Abraham which is meant to be rediscovered by you. Are you ready to receive your blessings?

CHAPTER 11 – THE ABRAHAMIC COVENANT

Seven Inheritance Promises – Seven Inheritance Words

Wisdom has built her house; she has set up its seven pillars.

--Proverbs 9:1, NIV

The covenant God made with Abraham had *seven* particular promised inheritances, which are the seven pillars that all covenant blessings rest. They were given one at a time and in a certain order. I think that was important, don't you? And get this; they were sealed with corresponding visible demonstrations or a word to make them easier to remember. These symbolic acts, accompanying the promises, became traditions passed down through generations all the way to Jesus and beyond.

Jesus upgraded these seven inheritances in the new covenant, which I have added to the promises of Abraham so you can benefit from both the old and the new. For better understanding, I have shared an example of my own experience that connected me to my *inheritance promise* in that specific situation. For easier recall, I reduced each of the seven promises to an *inheritance word* that starts with a "P." Graham Cooke says, "God will give you an inheritance word. The word will set you up to discover what you are going to experience during the next phase of your journey of faith." [27] Are you ready to get blessed, heir of God? These belong to you!

1) The Promise of *Partnership* [the Inheritance Word]

Then Melchizedek king of Salem brought out bread and wine.

--Genesis 14:18, NIV

The first promise God made to Abram (Abraham) was an offer to *partner* with him in the invisible realm and to become intimate with God Himself. This was mind blowing! Think about it. God wanted to partner with him in everything. Not just once, but eternally, every minute of every day. This was absolutely the most important promise of the seven. Without a partnership, the others could not exist. So how did God accomplish this partnership? I'm glad you asked. Of course, it was beyond brilliant.

Melchizedek the Priest (as covenant initiator) gave Abram (the covenant recipient) bread and wine and blessed him. Communion was the symbolic act of partnership. Abram gave the Priest a tithe, a tenth of his increase that came from the victory God had given him over his enemies.

Melchizedek means "King of Righteousness." He was also the King of Salem (Peace). He was both a priest and a king at the same time. "Without father, without mother, without genealogy, having neither beginning of days nor end of life but made like the Son of God, he remains a priest perpetually" (Heb. 7:3, NASB).

Who was this guy Melchizedek, who was a king and a priest without genealogy? Got a clue, yet? Some would say, "This can't be Christ because it was someone like him." I beg to differ. Christ was sometimes referred to in the Old and New Testaments as "like the Son of God" or "like the Son of Man." Here's the proof: "Lo, I see four men loose, walking in the midst of the fire, and they have no hurt; and the form of the forth is like the Son of God" (Daniel 3:25, KJB). There is no doubt that this was the pre-incarnate Christ in the midst of the fiery furnace. And again, "I saw in the night visions, and, behold, one like the Son of Man, came with the clouds of heaven" (Daniel 7:13, KJB). Oh yeah, no doubt here either.

What about these proofs in Revelation? "And in the midst of the seven lamp stands One like the Son of Man, clothed with a garment down to the feet and girded about the chest with a golden band" (Revelation 1:13, NKJV). Another quote reads, "Then I looked, and behold, a white cloud, and sitting on the cloud was one like a Son of Man" (Revelation 14:14, NKJV) So what do you think? Could this be Christ?

Even though controversial today, many Bible scholars, as well as most of the early church fathers, identified Melchizedek as the pre-incarnate Christ. This was Christ revealed in the old testament, as king and priest. Now tell me, my wise one, do you think that Melchizedek, who was *like the Son of God,* could actually be Christ? Obviously, according to scripture he could be! Only God had no beginning or end, was without birth or descendants, until the Son of God was born on the earth. He then had a beginning with a biological ancestry from Mary, His mother. Want more proof?

The Dead Sea Scrolls

The Dead Sea Scrolls verify who Melchizedek was. They referred to him as "Your Divine Being." Here is an excerpt: "With His coming, Melchizedek will return to the righteous ones what is rightfully theirs, and release them from debt of all their sins, and deliver all the captives from the power of evil, and by His might He will judge God's holy ones and all the peoples and so establish a righteous Kingdom"[28].

Did you see it? This *Priest* delivered the people from the power of evil and their sins, making them righteous, so they could get their inheritances. This *King* took pleasure in giving the holy kingdom to the people on the earth. Only Christ could do these things! Don't you agree?

This High Priest (Christ) made covenant with Abram by offering him bread and wine, representing His body and blood. They were now "blood brothers." By this act, the Old Testament patriarch and his descendants were connected to Jesus Christ. The communion with bread and wine was the symbolic act of Abraham becoming one with Christ so that the old promises to Abraham could be continued in the new covenant. It doesn't stop here. There were other important aspects to this intimate covenant union that were really cool!

The Sharing of Lives – No Secrets

Since an intimate *partnership* included the *sharing of lives* with one another, God would do nothing in secret that pertained to Abraham; thus, He shared His plans with him regarding Sodom and Gomorrah. The Lord said, "Shall I hide from Abraham that thing which I do?" (Genesis 18:17, NKJV). He wanted to show Abram what he was doing. Can you believe that! The God of the universe wanted to share His plans with the covenant recipient and was willing to change them if what Abram (or you) asked for was in agreement with His will. (Remember, he asked to save the city if ten righteous men lived there.)

Now get this, heir of Abraham. Christ even shared with Abraham the cross and resurrection that would happen thousands of years later. Why so? It was to show him that the promised blessings given to him would also come on Gentiles (see Galatians 3:14). Jesus said, "Abraham saw my day and was glad" (John 8:56, KJV). Long before the historical crucifixion was accomplished on earth, Abraham by faith stepped into the eternal realm where the cross already was. He embraced the cross and had fellowship with Christ in the person of Melchizedek, the High Priest of the new covenant.

And guess what? King David was in a covenant partnership with Christ and God also showed him the cross, the new blood covenant and resurrection. Why? Because this involved David's kingdom, and his throne that would be given to Jesus to rule from forever. (See Luke 1:32-33.) "He [David] foresaw and spoke about the resurrection of the Christ." (Acts 2:31, ESV). In Psalm 22, David writes about the agony of the cross.

Abraham learned to live by grace, not having to perform the rules and regulations of future Mosaic laws. And David also lived by grace, even while living in the midst of the law. Because of these eternal partnerships with God, Abraham and David were blessed in everything they did. Don't forget, heir of Abraham, these same blessings belong to you, the new covenant believer in partnership with Jesus Christ.

Realize the scope of this partnership, heir of God. Ponder this: the Trinity is your Senior Partner in everything! The Holy Spirit (who is one with Jesus; who is one with God) brings all three to live within you consistently, and will never ever leave you. Everything you will ever need is contained within this *partnership*, because all blessings are within you in the Trinity. God loves to share what He is doing with you, in you, and through you for your specific situation. Think on that!

The Symbolic Gesture for Partnership –Bread and Wine

Communion became the traditional symbolic act for a *covenant partnership* passed down throughout generations. It was believed that as the covenant parties partook of bread and wine together, they became a part of each other: "I in you and you in me." As each gave these elements to the other, and as it was ingested and assimilated into them, the two became one – unbreakable and partnered for life.

Here's an example: Two eggs are separate, divided entities, until scrambled (partnered) together. They then become as one. Try to separate them back into two entities from the one. It is impossible to do so. A marriage covenant partnership is just that--the two become scrambled together in God's sight. "And the two shall become one flesh" (Mark 10:8 NKJV).

CHAPTER 12 – THE NEW COVENANT

Jesus Continued the New Covenant Promise of Partnership

For we are all partners with Christ.

--Hebrews 3:14, GNT

God had partnered with Abraham through communion. It was no coincidence that prior to the cross at the Last Supper, Jesus performed this symbolic gesture for a partnership by breaking bread and drinking wine with His disciples. Jesus took bread and broke it, saying, "This is my body which is given for you." He took the cup and said, "This cup that is poured out for you is the new covenant in my blood" (Luke 22:19-20, ESV). "If you eat my flesh and drink my blood, you are one with me, and I am one with you" (John 6:56, CEV).

Like the wedding at Cana, Jesus saved the best wine for last. He took Abraham's promise from the old covenant and upgraded it (improved it, increased the quality, raised it to a higher standard). What was the upgrade? It was Christ *in you* and you *in Christ.* That was a colossal upgrade! The Holy Spirit comes to live *within* you as a habitation and to be with you forever. In the old covenant, God visited them and the Holy Spirit occasionally came *upon* them, then lifted off. What a difference!

When the disciples partook of the bread and wine, they knew it was an act of the blood covenant marriage relationship, but they had no idea that the Spirit of Christ would live in them. This "bride," however, was not about gender or sexuality, but about becoming the *recipient of the covenant*. The receiver would become *one* with the Lord, as joint heirs, with all the covenant benefits and blessings.

Even though the Lord's preeminence is distinctive from yours, God does not make the separation because you are one with the Son of God. When God looks at you, He sees His Son, and when He looks at His Son, He sees you. For instance, when Saul was persecuting the saints of God, Jesus asked Saul why he was persecuting Him. He always sees you as joint heirs, Christ in you and you in Christ.

Jesus was heir to the family business and fortune, and so are you. "As he is, so are we in this world" (1 John 4:17, KJV). Romans 8:16-17, NKJV says, "We are the children of God and if children, then heirs; heirs of God, and joint-heirs with Christ." You have access to the same infinite heavenly benefits, rights, resources, blessings, and responsibilities that Jesus had. Oh yeah!

And similar to any marriage, this partnership placed the bride into the family of the groom; thus, you were given the most blessed gift of having Jesus' Father as your Father. The followers had to be taught that, as sons and heirs, they were now to look to God as their Father. Prayers by a "son" were to be addressed, not to Almighty God, but to Abba Father. Jesus said to pray in this way, "Our Father, in heaven, Hallowed be your name" (Matt. 6:9, NKJV).

At first, this may have appeared to them to be almost heretical, because in the old covenant, people saw themselves as servants of God and never dared to call God, "Father." Only a son had that privilege. This new covenant partnership made them more than just servants with tasks to perform. They were indisputably sons; sons that serve their Father. Sonship with inheritances was the core and spirit of this new covenant only made possible by being one with the Son of God.

"Because you are sons, God has sent forth the Spirit of His Son into our hearts, crying, 'Abba, Father!'" (Galatians 4:6, NASB). "The servant abideth not in the house for ever, but the son abideth ever" (John 8:35, KJV). Did you see that? The son lives in the house forever!

Abba (Daddy) is the name Jesus came to reveal. Child of God, your relationship with God is that of a loving Father with His devoted child. Alan Vincent says, "This is not a wrong familiarity but an appropriate reverence and fear of His awesomeness; that He is both the Almighty - Creator of heaven and earth - as well as Abba Father; my daddy, my hero."[29]

This new covenant was not like the old covenant communion where two became one in theory. This was Jesus Himself making you one with Him--not in theory, but in truth and actuality. "This is my body which is given for you. This cup is the new covenant in My blood, which is shed for you" (Luke 22:19-20, NKJV).

The new covenant communion of bread and wine was about remembering that the cross reversed everything. He died to give you His life; He died to bear your sin and give you His righteousness; He died to take your sickness and disease to give you His health. "Who Himself bore our sins in His own body on the tree, that we, having died to sins, might live for righteousness – by whose stripes you were healed" (1 Peter 2:24, NKJV).

Do you realize, covenant partner, that by partaking of Jesus' body, you are recalling that He is one with you because of His death and resurrection? Thus, you have access to all He is and has. The Trinity lives inside you. God's perfect nature is living within you; therefore, you are pure, righteous, and in right standing with God. No shame, guilt, or condemnation here! And God is healthy, so you have His health living inside you. He came to give you life and more abundantly.

In the old covenant, God was with man sporadically. In the new covenant, God lives *within man.* His presence, life, nature, and power are *in you* and *with you* constantly and continually. What God wants to do on earth can now be done, not just *for you* but *through you.* You are not a spectator, but a participant and co-ruler with God. He wants to do everything with you and nothing apart from you. Can you believe it? He enjoys your company. I learned about this amazing aspect of a partnership quite by accident.

Personal Example of the Covenant Partnership - Surgery

The [inheritance] word [partnership] will set you up to discover what you're going to experience during the next stage of your journey of faith. [30]

--Graham Cooke

In 1997, I was told surgery was necessary for a large suspicious tumor on my ovary. If it was malignant, only a miracle could save my life. And wouldn't you know it, this came at a time when I had no insurance. One doctor after another declined to help me. "Where do I go from here?" I wondered. Panic set in, and I wanted to give up, but God didn't. Just then a friend called to give me her doctor's number. He didn't want to take me either, but suggested I try a certain doctor who had once helped a patient without insurance. After presenting my situation to him, he agreed to do the surgery for free.

Knowing that it was God's will to heal, I got all my prayer partners to pray for God to heal me, so I didn't need surgery. We quoted scriptures over and over. I was so confident in my belief, I made the doctor do another ultrasound the day before the scheduled surgery. When the news came that the tumor was still there, disappointment hit me hard, and fear rose up in me. Surgery was on for the next day.

I called my prayer partners to give new directions on how I thought it should be prayed, such as, "give great skills to the doctors, let there be no malignancy, a quick recovery, etc." Still, I had no peace, even though I knew these were good things to ask for. It was God's silence that was deafening and made me so uncomfortable. In the dark of the night, I went to Him and asked, "Father, what's wrong? I am standing on Your word. Why isn't this going as I thought it should?"

Without hesitation, His voice sounded loud but stern, "You haven't asked Me what I want to do in this particular situation!"

Those words pierced my heart as I realized I had made it all about me, directing God to do my bidding. He wanted to partner with me. I repented and requested forgiveness, asking Him, "What do You want to do in this circumstance? Who do You want to be for me, and what do You want me to do?"

I listened intently. Immediately Isaiah 60 flashed in my mind like a neon sign. As I was reading about His glory coming upon His people, I heard in my spirit, "This is what I want to do; to show my glory on you in the hospital. Will you partner with me in this?"

Silence.

Really? It made absolutely no sense, but I knew this wasn't something I dreamed up. Time to obey. I called my friends again to tell them, "This isn't about me. It is about partnering with God where He gets glory in it, through me." We all came into agreement and prayed from that perspective.

Check in the next morning brought an amazing unexpected surprise. When I told the receptionist what doctor I was scheduled to see, she smiled big and proceeded to tell me about him: "Do you realize who you have? Dr. DiSaia is one of three top cancer surgeons in the world. Doctor's and others come from all over the world just to get a glimpse of him, if even for five minutes. You are very blessed, indeed."

Wow! God had gone before me to give me the very best. But what about this glory He wanted to put on me? Yes, it came upon me while being prepped for surgery. I knew it by the responses of all that were witnesses there, including the anesthesiologist, the nurses, and the doctor. They tried to come up with words as to what they were seeing:

"You're glowing!"

"There is a brilliant radiance about you."

"Light is emanating from you."

"We've never seen a patient look like this before surgery."

God's glory made me desirable and beautiful. All were drawn to the glory on me and wanted to talk about it.

The surgery went perfectly, with no malignancy, little pain, and no need for the morphine that is always required afterwards. I recovered almost immediately. That night, alone in the darkness of my room, I thanked God for taking such good care of me, but I couldn't help but wonder why. Why did He want to do this? So, I asked, and He said, "My glory is coming upon my people in the appointed end times. I gave you a taste of it, so you can partner with me; pray for it in faith and expect it to happen."

"For behold, darkness shall cover the earth, and thick darkness the peoples; but the LORD will arise upon you, and his glory will be seen upon you" (Isaiah 60:2, ESV). "For as the waters fill the sea, the earth will be filled with an awareness of the glory of the LORD" (Habakkuk 2:14 NIV).

And glorious one, God wants you to know what He will do for you in every particular situation. To know His will, you must ask questions like, "What do You want to do in this? What are You doing for me, in me, and through me?" Then listen. When you find out His will, join in agreement with Him. If your will is different than His, guess who has to give it up? When you submit and surrender to God's will, only then can you partner with Him. Partnership means to agree with Him and act accordingly.

Having confidence in what He has said to you personally, you will be able to stand boldly to decree the truth and refuse to have less than what God wants and promised you. This is the time to behold the beauty of your God and to know His majesty with increased intimacy.

Let this sink in, child of promise, that the God of the heavens and earth—the One who made everything that exists, the One who is all powerful, all knowing, all good and all love—promised to partner with Abraham and now with you. He is your Senior Partner in everything! This covenant promise is not earned by works on your part but is received by faith when you partake of God's grace. It is a gift from God, and what a precious gift it is!

This was a partnership with the invisible. The greatest blessing you could ever receive is to be one with Christ. As the bride of the marriage covenant, you are also a child of Father God, empowered by God's Spirit to prosper. This partnership was not just about what God can do. We are told that Jesus was limited and could not do many miracles because of the people's unbelief. (See Matthew 13:58)

This was also about what you can believe, accept, and receive from Him, so He can do mighty works *through* you. Faith causes you to step out of time, into the realm where all that God has spoken into existence is available to you. Blessings are hidden, not *from* you, but *for* you in your heavenly account in another dimension. This is a joint-venture relationship, a divine exchange. Replace your fear with His love, your anxiety for His peace, your lack for His abundance.

Every situation you find yourself in has a promise with provision attached to it. This time, my *Inheritance Promise* was, "the LORD will arise upon you, and his glory will be seen upon you" (Isaiah 60:2, ESV). And my *Inheritance Word* was, "Partnership." When you find out God's will, you can stand on His promise in confidence, no matter what happens.

You must know that this truth is for you, partner of God. Believe it belongs to you, receive it as such, act upon it by releasing your faith, and expect God to confirm His Word. Say with confidence, "I believe I have received a partnership with Christ as the recipient of the covenant. I am one with Him. All He is, I am; all He has, I have. Because of this, I am joint heirs with Jesus, and His Father is my Father. This makes me a child and heir of God, and through this covenant, I have inherited the blessings of Abraham." Then, precious one, boogie! Dance your way happy.

CHAPTER 13 – THE ABRAHAMIC COVENANT

2) The Promise of *Protection* [the Inheritance Word]

Do not be afraid, Abram. I am Your shield.

--Genesis 15:1, NKJV

God calls Himself a shield. "Shield" means "protector, cover, an armed warrior of defense against judgments." [31] God Himself was Abraham's shield and the source of safety and protection, as well as the defense of any judgments or weapons formed against him. Now that should make you feel safe and secure, protected one. God surrounds you as a shield of protection!

Right away, "The Shield" began His role as protector. We see evidence of this when God kept Abram and Sarah from famine, and Sarah was protected twice from the captivity of two heathen rulers (See Genesis 12:10-20). Even Lot was rescued from destruction because of the covenant God made with his uncle Abram. Abraham's household was included in this promise of protection.

Moses

It was Abraham's great grandchildren that became the nation of Israel. When a famine arose, God sent them to Egypt. After a while, the Egyptians began to afflict them, but the more they did, the more the children of Israel multiplied. Taskmasters brought them into cruel bondage and began killing their newborn sons by casting them into the river. The cries of His people came up before God, and of course, He remembered the eternal covenant made with Abraham. He devised a plan to bring the descendants of Abraham out of Egypt (affliction) and into a blessing, the land of milk and honey (See Exodus 2:24).

What an awesome plan that was. The Lord told Pharaoh, through Moses, to let Israel go, but he would not. So, God sent plagues with frogs, lice, flies, boils, hail, and locusts as judgments against the gods of Egypt to confront the injustices. "The Shield" stood between His covenant people and the Egyptians. Not one plague was permitted to hurt the Israelites who were kept safe in Goshen. Still, Pharaoh refused to let them go, so God hardened the ruler's heart. Now maybe you are wondering why He did that. Perhaps it was so justice could be served for the killing of Israel's newborn sons. The final plague of righteous judgment would now come to all of Egypt's firstborn sons.

Moses went to Pharaoh, "Thus says the Lord: 'Israel is my firstborn [nation]. So I say to you, let my son go that he may serve Me. But if you refuse to let him go, indeed I will kill your son, your firstborn.'" (Exodus 4:22-3, NKJV) Pharaoh not only refused to release them but threatened to kill Moses should he see him again. Did this refusal play into God's plans? Oh yeah, big time!

The Passover

God's plan to save Israel from the death of the first born was brilliant. They were instructed to observe "The Lord's Passover." The people were to take an unblemished lamb for each household, kill, eat it, and apply the blood to the lintel and doorposts of their homes. Now check out how God chose to keep them safe: "For the LORD will *pass through* to strike the Egyptians; and when He sees the blood on the lintel and on the two doorposts, the LORD will *pass over* the door and not allow the destroyer to come into your houses to strike you" (Exodus 12:23, NKJV).

These words "pass through" and "pass over" are very important to examine. "Pass through" in Hebrew is "*abar*"– it means to cross through. And "Pass over" in Hebrew is "*pacach*" – it means "to hop" or "leap over" [32]

Did you notice, observing one, that God *passed through* the land to execute judgment against the Egyptians (See Exodus 12:12, 13). He *hopped over* the threshold of the door (a covenant act used in those times) to enter the house and "shield" the occupants, so death could not touch any of them. Perhaps, this was a type and shadow of the new covenant, when God's Holy Spirit enters into your house (body) to shield you. Don't you agree, beloved, that God's got your back?

When death claimed the lives of all the (uncovenanted) first born sons of Egypt, Pharaoh, in great anguish, cast out the Israelites. Now get this: God didn't let them go out empty-handed. Oh no! He gave them favor and they were abundantly rewarded by the Egyptians for all the years of hard labor performed without just compensation. They left with great wealth: gold, silver, jewelry, and clothing (See Exodus 12:35); therefore, don't worry about your injustices. God always sees and remembers everyone!

God's mercy redeemed them as they journeyed out of Egypt. He kept them safe by separating them from their enemies with a protective pillar of fire that gave heat and light to them by night. Then by day, God gave them a cloud covering that protected them from the sun's heat and also served as a guide for them. When the cloud moved, they moved; when it stopped, they stopped. Again I wondered, could the fire and cloud be like the Holy Spirit that lights the way to guide and lead you? What do you think?

The cloud happened to stop at the Red Sea, where they were hemmed in on all sides with no way out. Then *God prompted Pharaoh* and his army to pursue after the Hebrews. What was God, the Protector, thinking? It certainly appeared to be their demise when Pharaoh caught up to them, since they were like sitting ducks. Moses immediately began to pray, and what transpired next was a lesson for us all.

Josephus tells us the prayer Moses prayed to God,

> Thou art not ignorant, O Lord, that it is beyond human strength and human contrivance to avoid the difficulties we are now under; but it must be thy work altogether to procure deliverance to this army, which has left Egypt at thy appointment. We despair of any other assistance or contrivance, and have recourse only to that hope we have in thee; and if there be any method that can promise us an escape by thy providence, we look up to thee for it. And let it come quickly, and manifest thy power to us; and do thou raise up the people unto good courage and hope of deliverance who are deeply sunk into a disconsolate state of mind. We are in a helpless place, but still it is a place that thou possessest; still the sea is thine, the mountains also that enclose us are thine; so that these mountains will open themselves if thou commandest them, and the sea also, if thou commandest it, will become dry land. Nay, we might escape by a flight through the air, if thou shouldst determine we should have that way of salvation."[33]

Moses had assessed the situation. He knew it was beyond their strength or abilities, and that the people were beside themselves and inconsolable. Have you ever been there? Now it gets really good; Moses didn't look at the state they were in, but took a stand. He surmised that being stuck there was by God's hand and appointed of Him. He absolutely knew God was his protector and reminded Him that they wanted no one else to assist them, but God.

That meant he didn't think about what he had to do to remedy this. He didn't give a minute's thought of the power of the enemy, nor did he ask, "Where are you, God? Don't you care that we are in this cruel situation?" Nope, Moses knew they were in a helpless, hopeless situation, so he surveyed the mountains and the sea and looked for the way of escape from God's perspective. Then he added (and I love this), "Let it come quickly'" Oh yeah, like in two minutes.

You can't help but love this man Moses! No wonder he was chosen of God! He understood covenant; God had to protect His covenant nation because He said He would. I can just hear the Lord say, "OK, Moe, you're giving me a choice of mountains or the sea opening or flying through the air. I think the sea becoming dry land is a good idea."

Josephus continues on,

> Moses struck the sea with his rod, and receiving those waters into itself, left the ground dry, as a road and a place of flight for the Hebrews. He went first of all into it, and bid the Hebrews to follow him along that divine road and to rejoice at the danger their enemies that followed them, were in. The Hebrews got first over to the land on the other side without any hurt. [34]

Did you pick up on the wisdom of Moses? When the whole army was bearing down on them (you know, the ones on horses and chariots with weapons galore, yeah that army), the Hebrews began to flee through the path made in the sea. Moses then instructed his people to feel sorry for the Egyptians, because it was them who were in great danger. OMG! Who is this man, Moses?

Josephus continues,

> Whence the others were encouraged, no harm would come to them neither; but the Egyptians were not aware that they went into a road made for the Hebrews, and not for others; that this road was made for the deliverance of those in danger, but not for those that were earnest to make use of it for the others' destruction. As soon therefore, as ever the whole Egyptian army was within it, the sea flowed to its own place and came down with a torrent raised by storms of wind and encompassed the Egyptians. Showers of rain also came down from the sky, and dreadful thunders and lightning, with flashes of fire. Thunderbolts also were darted upon themselves. And thus did all these men perish. [35]

Child of God, did you see the biblical principal I saw? The way of escape from an ominous situation is to think this way: what the enemy means for your destruction is the very pathway of their impending doom, but for you, it is a divine road for your deliverance and blessing. You don't need to take my word for it. Here is God's word on it:

> And in no way be alarmed or intimidated [in anything] by your opponents for such [constancy and fearlessness on your part] is a [clear] sign [a proof and a seal] for them of [their impending] destruction, but [a clear sign] for you of deliverance and salvation, and that too, from God.
>
> --Philippians 1:28, AMP

The word "salvation" is from the Greek word *soteria*, which also means welfare, prosperity, safety, preservation, and health. [36]

Did you see a condition here? It is *"if"* you, like Moses, aren't panicked and maintain faith in God's deliverance, He will part the sea for you too. Graham Cooke believes that "God has allowed evil to come against us to lure them into a trap He has set for them." [37] Oh yes! And Graham says, "Every problem we encounter comes with His provision attached to it. Know God's promise and expect a provision. Every obstacle, every problem, every attack is allowed and designed to teach you to be more like Jesus. That's why every problem comes with provision attached to it." [38] I agree with him. Check out his teachings, they're superb!

Every problem comes with a promise and a way of escape, with provisions attached. So, click on the attachment already, faithful one! Find His word on it. Here is the proof of provision that finds you.

Josephus finishes with this,

> When they [Hebrews] found they had God so evidently for their protector and now having escaped the danger they were in, and seeing their enemies punished in such a way as never recorded of any other men whosoever, they were all the night employed in singing of hymns and in mirth. On the next day Moses gathered together the weapons of the Egyptians, which were brought to the camp for the Hebrews by the current of the sea, and the force of the winds assisting it; this also happened by Divine Providence that they might not be destitute of weapons. [39]

Don't you love Josephus for showing us the power of God and the wisdom of Moses?

God was the Hebrews' protector, and He will be your evident protector too, because you're in covenant with Him. Did you see how willing He was? God always does more than you can imagine. He even gave them all the weapons of the enemy by causing the sea current and wind to bring them to the Hebrews. God continued long after that to protect Israel in the wilderness by defeating any and all enemies that came against them. He kept them safe from diseases and there was not one sick or feeble among the millions of them (See Psalm 105:37, Deuteronomy 29:5). If God did this for them, how much more will He do for you, bride of Christ?

The Symbolic Gesture for Protection – Shield or Giving of Weapons

Throughout future generations, the person initiating the covenant would perform the promise of protection by giving his shield, belt, and/or weapon to the covenant recipient. This signified the promise of protection from enemies and harm, sharing all of his strength, and protecting abilities, and even to giving his life, if necessary. The promise also included the descendants. The initiator would say something like this, "Your enemies are now mine. Anyone who comes against you, comes against me. I will be for you and your descendants a shield and defense." And the recipient would receive this promise.

CHAPTER 14 – THE NEW COVENANT

Jesus Continued the New Covenant Promise of Protection

But the Lord is faithful, and he will strengthen you and protect you from the evil one.

--2 Thessalonians 3:3, NIV

The promise to Abraham was that God was His Shield, but Jesus upgraded it (improved it, increased quality, raised to a higher standard). What was the upgrade? In the new covenant, not only was God your shield of protection along with His angels, but now demons and devils were subject to you. Oh yeah! How did this happen?

Through the Cross, Jesus defeated Satan and took back the relinquished authority of Adam. He said, "All authority in heaven and on earth has been given to me" (Matthew 28:18, NIV). He then passed the authority on to you, "I give to you power [authority] to tread on serpents and scorpions and over all the power of the enemy, and nothing shall by any means hurt you" (Luke 10:19, KJV).

This was to be teamwork; the Trinity and you working together to thwart the works of the deceiver. No wonder demons tremble at the sight of you. The devil can only blow smoke because the One who already destroyed his works is with you. Your weapons of war are no longer physical, like a shield, but are spiritual. "For though we live in the world, we do not wage war as the world does. The weapons we fight with are not the weapons of the world. On the contrary, they have divine power to demolish strongholds" (2 Corinthians 10:3-4, NIV).

Your enemies are not human. They are evil spirits in heavenly places. Jesus showed you who your enemies really are, the spiritual forces that deceive to hold people captive. "This is not a wrestling match against a human opponent. We are wrestling with rulers, authorities, the powers who govern this world of darkness, and spiritual forces that control evil in the heavenly world" (Ephesians 6:12, GWT).

You have God's weapons to defeat every illegal act of the enemy. When attacked, your shield is the faith of God that you hold up above all of the other weapons. "At all times carry [His] faith as a shield; for with it you will be able to stop all the flaming arrows of the evil one" (Ephesians 6:16, CEV). The shield of faith is only one of God's weapons of warfare.

The sword that you wield is the Word of God, because the Word is encased in the belt of His truth, and the truth always exposes the lies. "You will know the truth, and the truth will set you free" (John 8:32, CEV). Your helmet is the salvation of God that protects your thoughts unto the saving of your soul. Your breastplate is the righteousness of God that protects your heart and who you really are. The shoes you wear are His peace. Peace rules and always treads over anxiety and worry. (See Ephesians 6:13-17)

You participate with your Covenant Keeping God to bring His kingdom principles, will, and order to earth wherever it is missing and anywhere the kingdom of darkness and evil forces prevail. It is God, the shining light in you, who overcomes the darkness. God never loses a battle, so that makes you a winner and an overcomer if you play by His rules. "You are of God, little children and have overcome them [the world]; because greater is He [God] that is in you, than he that is in the world" (1 John 4:4, NASB).

Overcoming Compared to *Giving up*

Overcoming obstacles is very important because Jesus overcame the world and wants you to do the same. The alternative to overcoming is quitting or giving up, and that's not how the kingdom operates. I remember a day that I wanted to quit everything. Have you ever been there? Problem after problem hit me in waves at a church where I was on staff. If that wasn't enough, my husband did a very hurtful thing, and I was done. That was that last straw--you know, the one that breaks the camel's back.

I cried out loud, *"I don't need this"* and stormed out. But where does one go to quit or resign from life? Really, I just wanted it all to go away. My bed had never looked so inviting, so I wrapped myself in a blanket, threw the covers over my head, and in a fetal position, fell instantly asleep.

I had a short dream that was life changing. In it, I was looking at an ominous, quivering, transparent pile that was dark and foreboding. I knew that the pile represented all my problems. I put my hands on my hips and shouted, *"I don't need this,"* and swiftly turned around to quit, but bumped right into Jesus. Uh oh – busted! Looking at the pile, He somberly asked me, "Lornah, do you want to know what to do with those?"

I quietly replied, "Yes, Lord."

He proceeded on, "Reach down and pick them up." As I did, the problems turned into a skirt. Then He ordered me, "Put them on." So, I did, and the skirt was a perfect fit. Then Jesus asked, "Did I say he who withdraws wins the rewards, or he who overcomes?"

Well, I knew the answer to that one, "Lord, You said, 'he who overcomes.'"

He replied, "Those problems are tailor-made for you to overcome. I strongly suggest you read Revelation, Chapter 2 - 3 about the rewards of overcoming." Immediately, I awoke.

While reading about the many rewards, I recognized what I would miss out on by quitting or running away from my problems. I got down on my knees, repented, and promised that I would never quit, unless Jesus told me to. I would go the distance! The desire to overcome every obstacle was established in me, and I trusted the One who overcame the world, as my Protector.

Mighty warrior, God wants to make you not just an overcomer but a conqueror and more. Not only do you conquer and get the victory, but you also get the spoils of the enemy, making him pay for the damage he caused you. "Now, in all these things [tribulation, distress, persecution, famine, nakedness, peril or sword], we are more than conquerors through Him who loved us" (Romans 8:37, NIV).

This war in the heavens is fought through prayer. When you speak God's Word in faith, in the authority of Christ's name, you become God's voice on the Earth. Angels are standing by to cause these words that you spoke in agreement with His will to come to pass. "Bless the Lord, you His angels, mighty in strength, who perform His word, obeying the voice of His word" (Psalm 103:20, NASB). Can you see yourself as God's voice, heir of God?

You can win every battle and thwart any attack if you don't quit, because the victory was already won on the cross. It will happen for you! So, don't pray to *get* the victory, but pray *from* the place of Christ's victory. You already have it if it agrees with His will and Word. The warring angels of God are backing you up. "Do not fear, for those who are with us are more than those who are with them. And behold, the mountain was full of horses and chariots of fire all around Elisha" (2 Kings 6:16, 17b, NKJV).

Sadly, many don't realize these important truths or who they are in Christ with the rights available to them through this new covenant. Protection and authority over your enemies are your covenant rights as a citizen of the kingdom of God and a member of His family. "You are therefore, no longer mere foreigners or persons excluded from civil rights. On the contrary you share citizenship with God's people and are members of His family" (Ephesians 2:19, WEB). "But we are citizens of heaven, where the Lord Jesus Christ lives" (Philippians 3:20, NLT).

American citizens have civil rights like health care, social security, police, and fire protection, but these benefits don't come automatically. To receive these rights, it's important that the citizens know how to activate them, such as filing the appropriate paperwork or dialing 911 in an emergency.

Likewise, citizens of the kingdom of God have similar legal covenant rights like heavenly protection, health care, economic wealth, resources, provision, blessings, and peace. To receive these benefits from heaven, you must know your covenant rights and activate them by believing and agreeing with God's Word, as well as by calling upon God to manifest His Word. The following is an example of activating my covenant right of protection.

Personal Example of Covenant Protection: a Car Accident

> The [inheritance] word [protection] will set you up to discover what you're going to experience during the next stage of your journey of faith.[40]
>
> --Graham Cooke

Several years ago, I was involved in a very serious car accident that should have taken my life. But before it happened, God in His goodness gave me a dream as a warning. In the dream, I was helping people get to safety from an attack of deadly snakes when a snake lunged at me and bit me in the leg. I knew the bite was fatal within an hour, as no one had ever survived this snake's venom.

Immediately, I tried to get to the ER, but no one would take me. Eventually I got there, and people were lined up with minor injuries waiting to see a doctor. Again, no one would let me go to the front of the line. I felt hopeless. Why wouldn't anyone help me when I was dying? As I waited, I fell into a state of despair. When I finally saw the doctor, he said, "There is nothing we can do to save you. How long ago were you bitten?" When I told him, he was shocked and confused that I wasn't dead.

He proceeded to examine me and found the reason. He said because I was in my menstrual period, the blood had washed away all the poison. Then, at that exact moment, the Lord entered the dream. He said, "Something is coming where no one can save you; not doctors or anyone; only the covenant blood. Don't forget to apply the protection power of the blood."

Sometime later, a young man lost control of his car on the freeway and spun around, crossing the lane in front of my car. I tee-boned him, head on, at over seventy miles per hour. A split second before the crash, as I saw the car coming in my peripheral vision, time shifted into slow motion. I assessed the potential seriousness of the situation. I knew that I didn't have enough time to slow down before the hit. This would mean that I probably would not wake up on this earth unless God intervened.

What came to my mind was the blood covenant promise of protection. I knew it wasn't my time to go home to heaven; I hadn't finished my course. I still had purpose to deliver on this earth; thus, I cried out to my covenant-keeping Protector, the One who never breaks covenant.

I heard the horrific sounds of crunching twisted metal, and then everything turned black. I passed out. When my eyes opened, my first thought was that I was alive! God was faithful to His covenant. Tears of joy streamed down my face as I thanked God for saving my life. As of yet, I didn't know the degree of damage the impact had done to my body.

The ambulance ride was painful. At the hospital the doctors discovered that I had no broken bones, only external bruising from seat belts and internal bruising of bones and organs from the force of impact—all things that would heal with time. The doctors were amazed that I lived. They wouldn't tell me the details about the other car, only that if he lived, he would be in the hospital for quite some time.

The Lord in His goodness verified what He had done for me that same week. During my recovery, I was watching the Discovery Health Channel. Two people were brought into an emergency room from an accident exactly like mine. This was a reality show and not a re-enactment. A young college athlete had tee boned an out-of-control car, head on, at forty-five mph. (The same collision as mine but I had hit at seventy-plus mph.) I watched as the doctors tried to save the life of both patients, but sadly they died. The doctors reported that the impact at forty-five mph was more than their organs could bear.

I wept as I realized the importance of believing and activating my covenant rights. God must have shielded my car, softening the impact at that high speed so death could not take me before my time. I thought about dying before finishing the course. Why would this happen? One reason is because of not discerning the Lord's body pierced and broken on the cross, or the covenant blood. Jesus paid a heavy price to give us the covenant rights of healing and protection along with all the benefits and privileges.

This is not about being perfect or unworthy when taking communion. It's about believing and thinking thoughts that agree with your covenant in Christ. "For he who eats and drinks [in communion] in an unworthy manner eats and drinks judgment to himself, not discerning the Lord's body. For this reason many are weak and sick among you, and many sleep [die before their time]" (1 Corinthians 11:29-30, NKJV).

Wow! Not knowing your covenant rights, Saint of God, makes you vulnerable like a sitting duck to demonic attacks. Satan's mission is to bring death and destruction. "The thief [devil] comes only to steal and kill and destroy; I [Jesus] came that they may have life, and have it abundantly" (John 10:10, NASB). Protection is included in your covenant rights. When you put a demand on God's word by speaking it in faith, heaven is under a covenant commitment to protect and deliver you and your seed.

Every situation you find yourself in has a promise with provision attached to it. This time my *Inheritance Promise* was, "But the Lord is faithful and he will strengthen you and protect you from the evil one" (2 Thessalonians 3:3, NIV). And my *Inheritance Word* was, "Protection." When you find out God's will, you can stand on His promise in confidence, no matter what happens.

These covenant blessings are available and accessible, but not automatic. God said not to forget the covenant benefits. So, the second promise for you to take as yours—to know, believe, and receive; to act upon and expect the results—is the protection God offers. That God Himself is your shield of protection and defense for you and your household. God promises to shield you from the destruction of evil, harm, accidents, sickness and disease, death, darkness, hell, and damnation. Remember that you have power and authority over all the power of the enemy. He is a defeated foe! Child of God, you are dearly loved and protected.

CHAPTER 15 – THE ABRAHAMIC COVENANT

3) **The Promise of *Position*** [the Inheritance Word]

Do not be afraid, Abram, I am your exceeding great reward.

--Genesis 15:1b, NKJV

Continuing in Genesis 15:1b (NKJV), God offered Abram a covenant of *position*. He said, "I am your exceedingly great reward." The Hebrew word, "reward" means, "worth, value, wages, benefit, a fitting compensation." [41] A reward is not a gift. It is being compensated for what you deserve; thus, God was saying to His friend, "I am what you deserve." Abraham's identity was now positioned in God and not in his own abilities.

Think on that! Abraham's significance, identity, and righteousness were not to be determined by his performance or toiling as a hired servant or a wage earner. It was to be solely based on his position in God and the irreplaceable value put upon him as a member of God's family. Did you get this, deserving one? You too have been made worthy of God. Selah!

The Lord made Abraham's name great, and he became a father of multitudes, positioned as heir of the world and a mighty prince among men. Kings would come through his lineage, and he was given great favor with both God and man. "For the promise that he would be the heir of the world was not to Abraham or to his seed through the law, but through the righteousness of faith" (Romans 4:13, NKJV).

Did you see it, seed of Abraham? By believing God's promises, you are heir of the world and have dominion over the things on the earth. Your descendants are leaders and rulers. You are not only an intimate friend of God, but in Christ you hold the upgraded position of joint heir with Jesus and son of God. It's your faith that has made you righteous, giving you favor with God.

This patriarch Abraham was royally robed with God's own righteousness, giving him right standing and position with God as His close companion and intimate friend. None other had held this position as God's covenant friend. "Abram believed the Lord, and he credited it to him as righteousness" (Genesis 15:6, NIV). And Isaiah described righteousness to be like a robe: "He [God] has covered me with the robe of righteousness" (Isaiah 61:10, ESV).

The Symbolic Gesture for Position - Giving His Coat/Robe

A covenant initiator would take off his coat or robe and put it on the beneficiary as a symbolic gesture for the *promise of position*. Just like a military officer's coat showed his rank and position, this act represented covering the recipient with his position, authority, honor, value, and worth. It was about upgrading the recipient's identity. The initiator would say something like, "I take off myself; all that I am and all that I have, I give to you. You now carry my position of honor and authority. My individual identity is given over to have a merged identity with you." As I am, you are!

Esther

A good example of getting a new position of royalty by receiving a robe is shown in Esther. The story began with Queen Vashti losing her royal position because she had usurped the king's authority and shamed him publicly. She was reduced to a concubine because of it. Her name meant "beautiful woman."

Perhaps her beauty was only skin deep. Possibly she was man's choice, instead of God's choice.

The king's commissioners gathered the virgins, including Esther, to bring before the king to find his replacement for Vashti. Esther's name meant "star." She was a shining light, beautiful inside and out. She was unknown and insignificant but that didn't matter. She was God's choice, and soon became the king's and the people's choice. "Esther obtained favor in the sight of all who saw her" (Esther 2:15, NKJV). And Josephus said, "The grace of her countenance drew the eyes of the spectators principally upon her." [42]

The king loved her above all women, and so he set the royal robe and crown upon her head. (See Esther 2:16-20.) Then sometime later, Queen Esther needed to come before the king to expose wicked Haman and save her people, but there was a huge problem. Josephus describes it this way, "Men with axes in their hands stood around about the throne in order to punish such as approached him [the king] without being called, and were killed immediately." [43] Esther had not been called in over thirty days.

Yep, that was one scary problem! After Esther fasted and prayed, she put on her royal apparel, and went into the king. Josephus wrote about what happened. When Esther came through the door, the king looked somewhat sternly at her and "her joints failed her immediately, out of the dread she was in, and she fell down sideways in a swoon." [44] Wow! I get it. Fear causes that swooning stuff. What happened next is so sweet and comforting. Josephus said that the king was so concerned for his wife that he leapt from his throne, took Esther in his arms, and embraced her. He told the queen that she should not expect anything bad by coming to him without being called. That law was made for servants, not the queen.

The king was in great agony over her being fearful, so he encouraged Esther to be of good cheer and to expect a better fortune since half of the kingdom belonged to her. He reminded her that she was joint heirs with the king and positioned next to him; seated on the throne. He wanted her to be secure in who she really was. He told her that she was queen, the same as he was king. Whatever she wanted in the kingdom, all she had to do was ask and he would grant her petition. [45] (Josephus Book of Antiquities)

Did you notice that only the covenant bride gets the crown and wears royal apparel, sits on the throne of the kingdom, and receives the inheritance? (That's why Abraham sent off his concubine Hagar and son, Ismael, without any inheritance. Sarah was Abraham's covenant wife, chosen by God.) Now think on this, joint heir of Jesus. You are positioned as Christ's queen (for you guys, it's "covenant recipient"). That means you are robed with His identity and crowned in His glory. You are loved above all others!

CHAPTER 16 – THE NEW COVENANT

Jesus Continued the New Covenant Promise of Position

And raised us up together [with Him] and made us sit together in heavenly places in Christ Jesus.

--Ephesians 2:6, NKJV

God covered Abraham with Himself, His position and worth, but how did Jesus upgrade this promise? Jesus positioned you together with Him permanently in heaven, as nobility. "And raised us up together [with Him] and made us sit together in heavenly places in Christ Jesus" (Ephesians 2:6, NKJV).

Now this should blow a few gaskets. Sitting next to King Jesus? Is this for real? It's hard to wrap your head around it because you are here on the earth, but this says that you are simultaneously positioned in heaven. You know that you will never be sovereign like God, obviously, but get this! You are in the same realm with God. Oh yes! For instance, like Queen Esther, you can also come boldly before your King Jesus, having access to His throne room anytime you want. "So let us come boldly to the throne of our gracious God. There we will receive his mercy, and we will find grace to help us when we need it most" (Hebrews 4:16, NLT). Why? Because you are the bride! Duh! Your covenant marriage makes you a joint heir with the rights to His Kingdom. Your kingdom is not of this world.

Jesus is the ruling King of kings and High Priest and heir of Abraham. As joint heir, you are given these positions. "Because as He is, so also are we in this world" (1 John 4:17, NASB).

"And [God] have made us kings and priests to our God. And we shall reign on the earth" (Revelation 5:10, NKJV). You are a servant king/queen with a royal priesthood—it is your inheritance.

Did you catch that, your highness? You rule as the co-heir with access to the king's resources. You reign from a position of authority in Christ in a spiritual kingdom, seated far above your circumstances at the right hand of acquittal, power, and blessing. "God has treated us with undeserved grace, and he has accepted us because of Jesus. And so we will live and rule like kings" (Romans 5:17, CEV).

Kings have power and authority to decree a thing, and it is established. And, as a priest, you serve God and represent Him by living a holy life, sacrificing for the good of others. This is who you really are!

Jesus was both the Lion King and the Priestly Lamb who sacrificed Himself for all mankind. Many don't realize who they are in Christ and live beneath their God-given callings. This is better explained through an intriguing tribal legend, which I have paraphrased. It goes something like this:

The Little Lion Who Thought He Was a Lamb

Once, while out grazing his sheep, a rancher heard a whimpering sound coming from the nearby bushes. To his surprise, it was a little lion cub that had been separated from the pride. Sensing danger, the rancher decided to keep watch from a distance. When the sun set, he feared for the cub's survival, so he brought him back to the ranch to care for him. He fed the cub and kept him warm, safe, and secure.

As the cub began to grow, he daily grazed with the sheep and became part of the flock. Accepted by the sheep, the little lion began to act, sound, behave, and smell just like them. He was a little lion who thought he was a lamb.

Months later, the little lion was grazing by the river with the sheep when suddenly from out of the nearby jungle appeared a large beast. His roar shook the ground and filled the atmosphere for miles. This creature commanded preeminence, and his aura of power and superiority was indisputable. The young lion had never seen or heard anything like it.

Terrified, the sheep and the little lion, who thought he was a lamb, dashed for the ranch and huddled behind the safety of the fence. Trembling and stricken in fear, they still could hear the creature making a sound so horrific that even the earth trembled with fright. As the little lion grew, he never forgot the sound that pierced his very soul.

When the young lion was fully grown, the herd of sheep ventured out to drink water from the river. As the young lion bent down to drink, he saw his own reflection in the water. He thought it was the beast! Panicking, he ran wildly toward the ranch. Why weren't the sheep running for safety with him? Hadn't they seen the beast that was in the water?

Slowly with time the little lion, who thought he was a lamb, risked rejoining his herd. Hardly had any time passed when out from the jungle came the terrifying beast again. The little lion froze as the sheep dashed for the ranch. This grand creature stepped in front of the young lion and the river. He raised his head and roared with a sound that was almost deafening as his razor-sharp teeth glistened in the sun.

The little lion thought his life was about to end, but sensed that the roar was saying, "Follow me." Hoping to save his life and appease the great lion, the little lion, who thought he was a lamb, tried to make the same sound. Trying as hard as he could, the only sound that came out was, "*Baaa.*"

The elder lion roared even louder, to which the young lion responded six or seven times with weak pathetic sheep noises.

Suddenly without warning, a growl came up from way down deep within the young lion and it sounded exactly like the elder lion's. And with that roar came a stirring within the little lion he had never experienced before.

The two lions kept roaring, one and then the other, as the younger echoed the elder. Suddenly, the ruling lion headed toward the jungle, but just before disappearing, he paused and looked at the young lion as if to say, "Are you coming?"

This was an invitation to become king of the jungle and to possess the spirit of a lion. The day of decision had arrived. The young lion had to choose whether to continue his life as a sheep, or to be who he had just discovered himself to be. To become his true self, he would have to give up the safety, security, comfortableness, and predictability of the simple life at the ranch and instead enter the unknown, untamed, dangerous life of the wild.

After looking back and forth from ranch to jungle, the little lion made up his mind. He turned his back on the ranch and joined the great lion to become who he had always been--a king and ruler of the jungle. He transitioned across the river from safety to discovery. He really was a lion all along, but he just didn't know it. It took the Great Lion to bring him to the truth. It was the King of lions who mirrored the life within--the life he was meant to live.

There comes a time—appointed of God—that you must shift from the safety of the herd to realized potential and possess the spirit of a ruler. You were a king all along, but just didn't know it. "It is God's privilege to conceal things and the king's privilege to discover them" (Proverbs 25:2, NLT).

Did you know God hides a man in a boy and a woman in a girl? He doesn't create the man or woman but hides them within. At the set time, you discover who you really are, as God mirrors Himself to you.

But before operating as a leader, you first must learn to be like sheep. They only follow and don't lead. When you learn to follow Jesus, to know the shepherd's voice, and become dependent on Him as the source for life itself, He calls you to become the person you really are in Christ. He shows you the life you were meant to live by upgrading your identity to be just like Him. Then your story makes you dangerous as you partner with Him in your new identity.

When you are fully under the authority of Christ, then your Father puts you in authority to rule over the things of the earth. "Now I say that the heir, as long as he is a child [infant, unlearned; simple minded, immature], differs nothing from a servant, though he be lord [owner] of all; but is under tutors and governors until the time appointed of the Father" (Galatians 3:29, 4:1-2, KJV).

Jesus Was Both the Lion and the Lamb

Jesus, as the Lion of Judah, was calling you to transition from being like sheep in the world to taking your rightful position as a king. Jesus was a King but had the heart of a servant. He became a sacrificial Lamb so that you could find your true identity as a servant king with a royal priesthood. You were made to serve others with the Kings' resources.

The center of heaven is the Lamb upon the throne, and the center of earth is the cross and the blood sacrifice. When you see Jesus in heaven, His stripes and piercings will be noticeable. His body will bear the markings of this great sacrifice made for you; however, Jesus was born a King. He will come back to the earth again, not as a Lamb, but as the King of (us) kings and the Lord of (us) lords.

"And I saw heaven opened, and behold a white horse; and He

that sat upon him was called Faithful and True. And He has on His vesture and on His thigh a name written, King of kings and Lord of lords" (Revelation 19:11, 16, NKJV).

If you do not know who Jesus Christ is and who you are in Him, you will live beneath the level and purpose God created you for. Dallas Willard says, "We all have the need to count for something, to be irreplaceable. The drive for significance is a simple extension of the creative impulse of God that gave us being. We were built to count. That is our destiny. Our hunger for significance is a signal of who we are and why we are here." [46]

God will show you, little lion, who He has made you to be. When you see yourself the way He sees you, and surrender to Him, you will begin to rise up to who you really are in Christ. There came a day when I sensed that the Lord wanted to reveal the spirit of the lion in me, and I wondered what that could mean? I knew the lion represented strength and honor, being confident, courageous, powerful, and secure in who he was--the king of the jungle. The time had come for me to possess the spirit of a lion.

Soon confirmation came when I happened to see a short TV video from Dr. Myles. He said something like this: We need to develop the attitude of a lion. A lion doesn't see himself through the eyes of realism. The reality is that he is not the biggest in the jungle (like an elephant), nor the strongest (a rhinoceros), he's not the fastest (like a cheetah), the tallest (a giraffe), the smartest (a gorilla), or the prettiest (like a black panther). But the lion doesn't see himself as "not enough." Instead, he sees himself as "more than enough," and is fearless in any situation. When a lion sees an elephant, he thinks, "lunch!" [47]

Did you get it, little lion? The lion is without limitations or intimidation because he knows who he is—the king of the jungle. He lives from who God made him to be and doesn't question it. He reduces the giant elephant as bread to eat, one bite at a time. Now it may take a while for the elephant to fall, but "the bigger they are, the harder they fall," Right?

This made me think about the story about Joshua and Caleb. Twelve spies had gone into the Promised Land and noticed it was full of giants much bigger than they. Ten spies gave an evil report: "We even saw giants there, the descendants of Anak. Next to them we felt like grasshoppers, and that's what they thought, too!" (Numbers 13:33, NLT).

Bill Winston says an evil report is anything spoken contrary to the covenant or God's word. This kind of report gives place to the devil to destroy and redirect your future. We live in a word planet, which was created by words and it was to be maintained by words. [48]

Now look at the humongous difference of the good report that Joshua and Caleb gave, "Only do not rebel against the LORD. And do not fear the people of the land, for they are bread for us! Their protection is removed from them, and the LORD is with us; do not fear them" (Numbers 14:9, ESV). Did you see it? They reduced the giants to bread to eat, one bite at a time. Speaking God's truth created their future.

The words of the ten wimpy spies influenced the people negatively, and their futures of living in the Promised Land were cut off. Only those under twenty years of age were able to enter. The two spies, Joshua and Caleb, went in because they put their faith in God who was greater than any giant in the land. They saw the giants as grasshoppers, like helpless prey, compared to their covenant keeping God.

Young lion, did you see how important it is to know who you are, to have the attitude of a lion and the mind of Christ about you? When you give into fear and see yourself as a victim of circumstances (a grasshopper), next to your giant problem, others will also see you that way: weak, pathetic, and pitiful.

Always see your identity upgraded from the old way of thinking. When you default to the old man—wimpy, insecure, emotional, fearful, or unlovable—download a new app. Replace the old life with the resurrected new man. Upgrade your identity to be like God.

The world tells you that not being enough is a bad thing--not being smart enough, not strong enough, not pretty or handsome enough, etc. Now contrast this to being in Christ, in covenant and in the Kingdom where you are more than enough. You are running a race, not to compete with others but to discover your potential—your real self.

It's time to run with the lions and face your fears, as well as to run to the roar and not from it. We need to develop a whole new attitude, to change our belief system from who I was (the wimpy guy), to who I really am (bold and courageous). When difficult situations come, see them as opportunities to practice being a new creation. Jeez, we're not just trying to survive. We are on an assignment to discover Jesus, the Lion of Judah within us.

Your journey and mine is not only about learning to release the Lion of Judah (strength and honor) from within, but also to exhibit the Lamb of God (meek and quiet spirit) at the proper times. If we stay in the emotions of the past, those feelings will keep us as sheep; unable to rule like a king of the jungle. If we keep trying to control difficult situations, those actions will make us as harsh kings. (I wrote about this as an allegory called, "The Lambhearted Lion," which is in the Epilogue of this book.)

Jesus gave us several positions. We are kings, priests, sons and heirs of God, Jesus, and Abraham, to name a few. God is faithful to teach us how to live in these positions. I want to share a special event that happened to help me learn more about being an heir of Abraham. I hope you enjoy it.

Personal Example of Covenant Position: a Trip to Israel

> The [inheritance] word [position] will set you up to discover what you're going to experience during the next stage of your journey of faith. [49]
>
> --Graham Cooke

I heard God's voice and recognized His presence. I was visiting a church to hear guest speaker Brian Simmons, and during his sermon, he mentioned he had one seat left on an up-and-coming trip to Israel. I knew I couldn't go, because earlier that day, I had loaned all my savings to my daughter to fix an urgent problem. This made it impossible to go; yet, unexpectedly, I heard that voice. The Lord said, "Go. I am sending you."

I kept arguing quietly with God, "I can't go. Surely, You don't want me to go into debt."

He was unrelenting and sternly stressed, "Sign up now or never." I felt the urgency and left.

I filled out the application online but delayed paying the money because I didn't have it. Was I hearing correctly? I began to doubt it was God, so I asked Him for a confirmation. He gave me two. Suddenly I was reminded of a friend who, two months before, out of the blue gave me a prophecy, "God says get your passport ready. In a couple months, He is sending you out of the country." At the time, I dismissed it as a misguided word.

The next day during the church service at Bethel, Pastor Eric Johnson said in his sermon,

> "Sometimes God is taking you deeper to trust Him and to get rid of the idols of your heart. An idol is anything you check with before obeying God. It could be

> like Him asking you to give all your money away and to trust Him. Then He asks you to do something but you look at the empty bank account and say I can't. God says, 'do it now or never.' Jump in all the way. He will supply what you need."[50]

OK, now I knew God would pay for what He ordered, but I wondered how He would do it. I went by a strong inclination I had to put it on my credit card. OK, I thought, this would give God thirty days to pay it off. I called the travel agency, but they didn't take credit cards. *What should I do now?* Was this resistance from God or the devil? I decided to call the credit card company to explain my dilemma.

The customer service rep left the phone to talk with higher ups. The conclusion was that I could write a check from my credit card account and they would charge zero percent interest for a year with no penalties. Wow, now God had a year to pay it off--which, by the way, He did. One day before the year's deadline, I got a check in the mail for the full amount. But that's another miracle story. God is so faithful!

Why was God sending me to Israel? What was his purpose? I had to know, so I spent time seeking Him. Someone just happened to send me a YouTube video on the Jews returning to their land in1948. In it, God had told the Jewish people that the land assigned to them would remain desolate as long as it was occupied by strangers and they were in exile. It thus remained a bleak, barren, undeveloped land for over 2000 years until their return. Then something amazing happened as written in an Israeli post: "From the deep sleep of oblivion, in the absence of its sons and daughters the land would finally awaken."[51]

(Israel Ministry of Foreign Affairs)

Prior to the Jews return, empires had tried to get the arid land to produce, but try as they may, they couldn't. The land seemed to know the rightful heirs and only yielded its increase for them. That made me think about the creation groaning, waiting for the revealing of the heirs (sons) of God that have legal right to the earth and their inheritances. (See Romans 8:19-22)

My thoughts were interrupted by that familiar voice. God said, "I made you a child of Abraham and heir of the blessings I gave to him. When you stand on Israel's land, stand in that position as an heir of Abraham, blessed to be a blessing. The land will recognize your position in this lineage as a rightful heir because in Christ, you've been grafted into Abraham's genealogy. I want you to see yourself in Abraham's family tree."

Oh my! I wasn't to go as a spectator or tourist, but as a descendant of Abraham. God gave me other wonderful things to do when I got there, but this one stood out among the others. What followed later was mind-blowing! The tour took us to a high-tech museum called Friends of Zion that had just opened in downtown Jerusalem. The intent of FOZ was to celebrate the Christian friends of Israel.

Upon entering, we passed by a camera and each of us had our picture taken--for security measures, I thought. At the end of touring the museum, we were taken to The Promise Theater. It was a virtual 3-D like theater. On the huge screen, there appeared an amazingly beautiful tree, its branches waving in the wind. In the background spewed a beautiful orange sky at sunrise.

The ancient, gnarled trunk of the tree came into full view, but wait, the gnarls began warping into a face. The face was the patriarch Abraham, but then it turned into Isaac, then Jacob, Moses, David, and so on. After this, the ancestry tree began shooting pictures of faces out from its branches and they were moving right towards us. Suddenly, right in front of my eyes, there I was as a descendant of Abraham! I could hardly believe it.

The picture grew bigger as it floated right in front of my face, seemingly only inches away. I was actually seeing myself in Abraham's family tree. This was exactly what God inspired me to do, to see myself as his heir. It wrecked me! It was like I had stepped back in time and the truth that God had positioned me as an heir of Abraham hit me hard. I got it! This was who I really was. Tears ran down my cheeks as I was consumed in the goodness of God. Being an heir of Abraham was a big deal! There were many blessings attached to it.

And the blessings didn't stop there. We were taken to the Jordan River to be baptized in the same place where Jesus was. As I came up out of the water, a memory came to me about an incident that had occurred several months earlier. I had invited a few friends to come to my house New Year's Eve and share with each other what we thought God was going to do in 2015.

My perception was that God wanted us to see ourselves possessing our promised inheritances according to Deuteronomy. "For you shall cross over the Jordan and go in to possess the land which the Lord your God has given you, and you shall possess it and dwell in it" (Deuteronomy 11:31, NKJV). To prophetically act this out, we all lined up and leaped over an imaginary line, symbolizing crossing over the Jordan and moving into our inheritances. We all shouted the victory.

Now, I could hardly believe it. A few months later, I was literally in the Jordan River! Isn't that just like God! I took the opportunity to swim across to the other side and back, declaring what belongs to me. Without a doubt, God's fingerprints were all over this trip: the last seat on the tour of 2015, the credit card, the museum opening its doors a couple months prior to arrival, and seeing the family tree of Abraham and myself as his heir. Then there was the prophecy of crossing the Jordan that God gave me for 2015--something I never imagined would become a literal reality. I am more than amazed at the majesty and goodness of my God!

Heir of Abraham, all that Jesus Christ is and has belongs to you. Don't let anyone steal from you who God has made you to be through the covenant: a joint heir with Jesus; a son of God and heir to His Kingdom; and an heir of Abraham's blessings. God called Himself the God of Abraham, and He is the God of you also. You are placed in His Kingdom with purpose and destiny. That position of heir that you carry is valuable and irreplaceable. Don't ever think thoughts that don't agree with your position and the value God has placed on you. This is your new identity!

Every situation you find yourself in has a promise with provision attached to it. This time my *Inheritance Promises* were, "So all who put their faith in Christ share the same blessing Abraham received because of his faith" (Galatians 3:9, NLT). "And [God] raised us up together [with Him] and made us sit together in heavenly places in Christ Jesus." (Ephesians 2:6, NKJV). My *Inheritance Word* was "position." When you find out God's will, you can stand on His promise in confidence, no matter what.

The third promise for you to take as yours—to believe and receive, to act upon, and to expect the results—is a position of royalty and right standing with God and men. You have nobility, honor, authority, and favor with God as a member of His family. Take hold by faith. You have a new identity in Christ!

(In the epilogue of this book is my story called "Song of Innocence" written in the captivating prose of Song of Solomon. It's about how God took me from a past of victimization to a whole new identity. Also included is an allegory called "Lamb-hearted Lion" that is about balancing strength and honor with a meek and quiet spirit, and how to be both the lion and the lamb simultaneously. Change how you see yourself and gain a new identity.)

CHAPTER 17 – THE ABRAHAMIC COVENANT

4) The Promise of Pardon [the Inheritance Word]

Bring me a heifer, a goat and a ram, each three years old, along with a dove and a young pigeon.

--Genesis 15:9, NIV

To assure Abraham that all of God's covenant promises to him would come to pass, blood had to be shed. Without it, there could be no eternal covenant. Before Jesus, animal sacrifices were needed to pardon sin and to establish the covenant; thus, the Lord said to Abram, "Bring me a heifer, a goat and a ram, each three years old, along with a dove and a young pigeon" (Genesis 15:9, NIV).

God had offered Abraham a pardon through the blood sacrifice of animals to forgive his sins through this unconditional blood covenant. He was made righteous because of his faith: "Faith was counted to Abraham as righteousness" (Romans 4:9, ESV). All of his sins, faults, and weaknesses would be forgiven; put under the blood covenant pardon.

These animals—the birds of the air and the animals of the land—represented heaven and earth coming together in an eternal agreement. The shedding of blood demonstrated that if this covenant was broken, the one breaking it had to die just like the animals. "Abram brought all these to him, cut them in two and arranged the halves opposite each other; the birds, however, he did not cut in half" (Genesis 15:10, NIV).

This was an eternal covenant. God didn't want to take any chances that Abraham might break it later, affecting generations to come. If he broke it, he would have to die. The blessings of Abraham would not be connected to the new covenant, and you and I would miss out. Can you see how crucial this was? God was thinking of you all this time.

In the custom of making a covenant, both parties would walk through the blood. This normally would have been God walking through it with Abraham, but no, that was not the case here. Instead, God put Abram into a deep sleep. I think he could still hear and see what was going on but could not participate. Then Jesus Christ took Abram's place as He walked through the blood with God. You might be wondering how God's Son could legally be the substitute for Abram. Well, I'm glad you asked.

This is too cool. Are you ready for this? Christ could do this because He and Abram had become one by the bread and wine of the Melchizdek partnership. Oh yeah! Remember that? This is why Jesus Christ could now take Abram's place and walk through the animal halves with God. God and Christ passed through the blood twice, signifying that God would maintain His part of the covenant and – don't miss this– Christ would keep Abraham's part forever. Oh yeah! Now the only one required to pay the penalty if broken was God or Christ. Like that could ever happen!

Can you imagine what Abraham saw? God the Father and the pre-incarnate Christ walking through the blood in the form of a figure eight through the halves. How does one describe this? Here's Abram's take on how he saw it: "And it came to pass, that, when the sun went down, and it was dark, behold, a *smoking furnace*, and a *flaming torch* that passed between these pieces" (Genesis 15:17, ASV). What? Why this description?

Elsewhere in the Bible, God was described as fire and smoke.

"Now Mount Sinai was all in smoke because the LORD descended upon it in fire; and its smoke ascended like the *smoke of a furnace*" (Exodus 19:18, NASB). Jesus was called light and His eyes were like *flaming torches* (Daniel 10:6, NASB). What Abram saw was indeed God, the Smoking Furnace and Jesus, the Flaming Torch.

This was now an unbreakable covenant that would be extended from Abraham to Jesus, through Jesus to His disciples, and then to you and me. This was a type and shadow of the new covenant that Jesus would bring many years later, when He would become your substitute, take your place on the cross, and pay your debt to sin. As Christ kept the covenant for Abraham, He would also keep your part of this unconditional covenant through His Holy Spirit living within the believer. How genius is this!

The Symbolic Gesture for Pardon – The Shedding of Blood

Covenants were always sealed through the act of shedding blood. Sacrificial animals without blemishes were prepared to atone for man's sin. (Remind you of anyone?) The animals were cut in half and placed beside each other. Just as two halves, though separated, were still one animal, so two covenant partners, though separate entities, would become as one.

The initiator and recipient would face each other and walk through the blood between the halves in a figure eight—eight as a sign of infinity demonstrating a covenant without end. This eternal agreement was called the "walk of blood" or "trail of blood." The two parties would stop in the middle, and the initiator would pronounce the blessings and pledge of loyalty in keeping this covenant. They would walk a second time and stop in the middle for the pronouncement of curses if this covenant should ever be broken. Next, both swore with an oath to God as their third-party witness to keep this covenant upon penalty of curses and death.

Some "cut the covenant" by cutting their wrists or hands and tying their wrists together so the blood would intermingle, which was another sign of two becoming one. As "blood brothers," they had a scar of remembrance. (Remind you of anyone with scars on His wrists?) That scar represented giving one's life for the other, dying to independence, and separation. All sin, faults, and weaknesses would be forgiven and under the blood covenant (pardoned forever).

The Importance of a Blood Covenant

A blood covenant relationship was more important than any other. You've heard the saying, *"blood is thicker than water,"* meaning that the biological family is more important than any other relationship. This is a distortion of the truth. Even though family is important, there is a higher priority. This saying really means that the blood covenant relationship always takes precedence over family relationships, those who are born from the water of the womb. Thus, blood is thicker than water. Bet you didn't know that, inquiring one!

A Middle Eastern expression is *"blood is thicker than milk,"* meaning that the blood covenant partnership is more important than the natural family, those who have sucked milk from the mother's breast. Even Jesus verified that a covenant relationship was a higher priority than family. He said, "For whoever does the will of my Father in heaven he is my brother and sister and mother" (Matthew 12:50, NKJV).

CHAPTER 18 – THE NEW COVENANT

Jesus Continued the New Covenant Promise of Pardon

So now there is no condemnation for those who belong to Christ.

--Romans 8:1, NLT

The promise to Abraham was that he was pardoned of his sin by the animal sacrifice. How did Jesus upgrade this? He Himself became the sacrifice, the spotless Lamb. All the sin of mankind was put upon Him so that you might be free from sin's grip and free from condemnation and guilt forever. "Blessed is the person whose disobedience is forgiven and whose sin is pardoned" (Psalm 32:1, GWT). His blood shed for you averted that judgment and made you righteous forever. Can you see what a great blessing it is to be pardoned?

On the cross, a divine exchange took place. "For He [God] hath *made* Him [Jesus] to be sin for us, who knew no sin; that we might be *made* the righteousness of God in him [Christ Jesus]" (2 Corinthians 5:21, KJV).

Check this out! Jesus was *made* sin and you were *made* righteous. The first word, "*made,*" (*poieo*) in Greek means "*appointed, to bear.*" It denoted a temporary act. Being *made* righteous is different. This word *"made"(ginomai)* means "*born, become, come into being, to be married.*"[52] It signified a permanent position. This was what it meant: Jesus was made sin one time only, so you could be made forever and eternally righteous.

What was the divine exchange? It was sin for righteousness. Righteousness is the ability to stand in God's presence and fellowship without guilt. What a deal! You are forever in right standing with God and because you're righteous, you inherit the Holy Spirit of promise, the pledge or guarantee of your inheritances. (See Ephesians 1:13,14, NASB)

In the same way that God "*made*" you male or female, which is something you are regardless of what you do, God has "*made*" you righteous, which is something you are that's separate from your behavior. It is a gift. You didn't earn it by works and can't lose it by your conduct or behavior. In other words, you are no longer a sinner saved by grace. Yes, prior to salvation you were identified as a sinner.

Afterwards when God's grace pardoned you, making you righteous, you were emancipated from sin and made totally new. "Therefore if anyone is in Christ [in covenant], he is a new creation: old things have passed away; behold, all things have become new" (2 Corinthians 5:17, NKJV).

"Sinner" is no longer a position or identity you carry; that is *NOT* who you are—it is who you once were. God can't bless sin; thus, when you occasionally sin, it can cause you to forfeit the benefits and blessings of the covenant. This, however, does not change your relationship with God. You are still His child. It can, however, affect your fellowship with Him. For instance, when your child sins, does he stop being your son? Of course not! He is still related to you forever. He may get a consequence or a time out that can disrupt his fellowship with you and stop his blessings for a while. Similarly, when you sin, God always looks to forgive and restore the benefits and blessings back to you when you repent.

No sin is worth losing your blessings, no matter how pleasurable it may be at the time. If you have sinned (transgressed) against another, confess the totality of the sin to God; then go to them and ask forgiveness. Grace was never meant to overlook sin. Since sin separates you from the Lord and others, it needs to be repented of and removed so that you may get back in the blessings. "The kind of sorrow God wants us to experience leads us away from sin and results in salvation [welfare, prosperity]. There is no regret for that kind of sorrow, but worldly sorrow which lacks repentance, results in spiritual death" (2 Corinthians 7:10, NLT).

What is repentance? Perhaps, this is a different slant on it. The word "repentance" means "change your mind and conduct; turn around."[53] The prefix "re" means "back again." And "Pent" means "top or highest position" (like a penthouse). To repent means to turn around and come back again to the highest position in Christ.

When you have messed up, let grace convict you through the Holy Spirit to godly sorrow. Repent, turn from sin, and change the way you think and align yourself with your new identity. Come back again to who you really are in Christ; the righteousness of God in the highest position as heir of the kingdom's blessings and benefits. Turn back to your Father. Be a quick "re-penter." Get back in His glory and blessing! When Jesus began His ministry, His first words were, "Repent: for the kingdom of heaven is at hand" (Matthew 4:17, KJV). In other words, righteous one, change your thinking about how you've done it in the past and turn to the kingdom of God. Here's a great example. You'll love it!

Repentance – The Farm

Dallas Willard gives a great explanation of this in his book, "The Divine Conspiracy." I have paraphrased, and it goes something like this: There was a poor farm family that had no electricity, until one day power lines were run to it. The power that could make their lives far better was right there, near them. By making relatively simple arrangements, they could utilize it and their lives would be vastly changed for the better.

The farmer had heard the message, "Repent, for electricity is at hand." Repent and turn from kerosene lamps, wood-burning stoves, scrub boards, sickles, and hoes. Turn from darkness to light and to a whole new way of life with lamps, refrigerators, microwaves, washers and dryers, tractors, and combines.

The farmer had to believe in the electricity and take the practical steps involved in relying on it. He had to turn from the lesser to the greater. Electricity had been made available to him, but the choice to repent was entirely his. He could stay with what he had always known and miss out on the benefits, or he could turn from the past and take hold of a whole new world.

Repentance is a call to reconsider how we approach life. First, it is turning from the lesser things, the root sins of an independent, self-righteous, self-sufficient, self-governing life. Then it is coming back to the greater things, to the kingdom of God with all the covenant benefits, rights, and blessings. [54]

Remember Adam? He was designed to live in heaven's atmosphere but fell from the higher life to a lower life. It is time to repent and come out of the pigpen into the palace penthouse, seated in heavenly places. Return to the top. Jesus paid the price once and for all for any sin you have committed or ever will commit. God sees you through the covenant blood; therefore, forgiveness is always yours if you happen to sin.

You are no longer a sinner. Jesus made you righteous. Trying to obtain righteousness by your own good works causes you to miss out on the grace of God. "For if you are trying to make yourselves right with God by keeping the law, you have been cut off from Christ! You have fallen away from God's grace" (Galatians 5:4, NLT).

Righteousness is not obtained through asserted willpower nor earned by trying to be good enough through the works of the flesh. "For they being ignorant of God's righteousness, and going about to establish their own righteousness, have not submitted themselves to the righteousness of God" (Romans 10:3, KJV).

Being made the righteousness of God defies verbal explanation. It is indefinable and stirs the emotions to exuberant joy because your earthly body is crowned with heaven's splendor. Your security is not based on performance but is based on your relationship with God and the pardon that comes with that partnership. It's not about your "do" but about your "Who." It's not what you did, but what Jesus did.

Through the new covenant, you were made one with God. (See Hebrews 10:14.) You are a spirit, have a soul which is your mind, will, emotions. You live in a body (five senses). In covenant with Christ, perfect one, your spirit became one with the Holy Spirit, and you took on the perfect nature and righteousness of God in your spirit. (See Hebrews12:23.) Your soul (thinking) needs to be renewed by the Word of God, and the lusts of your flesh brought under the power of the Holy Spirit. Ya think?

When Satan rebelled, he was relegated to live in darkness in the absence of God who is light (See 2 Peter 2:4). If we accommodate darkness through the tolerance of sin, we are vulnerable to satanic assault because Satan has legal right to dwell in darkness. So, bright one, don't give him access. Access comes not to your spirit but to the darkness of your soul and your self will, wrong thinking, and lusts of the flesh. This results in things such as fear, unbelief, envy, pride, lying, promiscuity, adultery, fornication, etc.

Did you know that what you focus on is attracted to you? Don't major on the wrongs but be mindful of the righteousness God has given to you, so that sin will not have mastery over you. "Awake to righteousness and sin not" (1Corinthians 15:34,

KJV). That means to reckon the wimpy old man, dead and buried. Remember who you really are and come back to that amazing righteous new person in the image of Christ. Come back to who you really are!

Receive the grace to repent and fully repent, turn away from it, re-calibrate, and get back under the benefits and blessings readily available to you. Pray something like this when you sin:

"Lord, I am so sorry that I sinned against You by not receiving Your grace. This is not who You made me to be; who I really am. I turn from the sin (name it) to the righteousness of God in Christ Jesus. I turn from anxiety (the sin) to receiving Your peace (the antidote for the sin). Thank You, Lord, that my sin, judgment, and punishment was paid for on the cross, and I am a new creation in Christ."

You don't have to go through a long ordeal of paying a price. David committed adultery, the consequences of which resulted in the loss of his first born from Bathsheba. His *full* repentance though changed some of the outcome. The very night of losing his son, God opened Bathsheba's womb and restored to them a son named Solomon, heir to the throne.

Remember, your majesty, you are a king and heir to the throne also. If you've messed up, repent promptly, and if someone else messes you up, forgive quickly. Get back under the blessings. Here's a good example of a situation I had with my mother.

Personal Example of a Covenant Pardon: Mom's Home Going

> The [inheritance] word [pardon] will set you up to discover what you're going to experience during the next stage of your journey of faith. [55]
>
> --Graham Cooke

I never had a close relationship with my mom but longed for one. She lived in her own world and seemed uninterested in mine throughout my childhood. No matter what I did, it was never enough. As an adult, I pressured her at times to try to get some kind of response from her, but nothing changed. She remained distant and unavailable. I even started arguments to get her attention, but each time I left to go home, anger overtook me. I felt rejected and unloved. Was this to be my fate for the rest of my life?

After giving my life to the Lord, He delivered me of this. It began when God spoke to me in the midst of my complaints about her. I was expecting Him to console me, but instead He said something like this: "Rather than focusing on what you don't have, or who she can't be for you; why don't you focus on what you do have and what I want you to do in this situation?"

At first, I was disappointed that His response wasn't about changing her, but I did want to know what God wanted me to do. Immediately, a very strong impression came that I was to search the Word about my responsibility before God with my mother and let Him deal with her. A feeling of conviction came over me as I diligently sought after what would be a child's obligation to their parent.

These scriptures stood out: "Children, obey your parents in the Lord for this is right. Honor your father and mother – which is the first commandment with a promise so that it may go well with you and that you may enjoy long life on the earth" (Ephesians 6:1-3, NIV).

Two words stood out: *"obey"* and *"honor."* My first thought was that this certainly didn't apply to me because I was an adult and didn't have to do whatever she asked of me. I sensed the Lord concurred but felt compelled to look up the original Greek meaning of each word. "Obey" (*hupakouo*) from *"hupo"* ("under") and *"akouo"* ("to hear") meant "to hear under as a subordinate; to listen attentively and intensively; to be fully responsive." And the word "honor" (*timao*) meant "to value at a high price; to esteem precious by the beholder." [56]

Wow! "Obey" had a completely different meaning than I had thought. God's mandate was very clear. My responsibility before God was to listen attentively to my mother, place a high value on her, and esteem her precious because she was chosen by God to be my birth mom. My mother and I were responsible before God to do what He required in our roles and not what we demanded of each other.

I also realized that these stout commandments didn't give me an out if she didn't do her part. There was no excuse for me not doing mine. It was time to give up trying to change her. Surprisingly, instead of feeling disappointed, I felt elated. Yeah, this was something I knew I could do!

Purposing to excel in it, I couldn't wait to do my part, but first I repented for becoming offended and losing my peace. I had lost it while trying to get her to meet my needs by making her do what she couldn't or didn't want to do. God's word comforted me, *"Even if my father and mother abandon me, the LORD will hold me close."* (Psalm 27:10, NLT) After that, I forgave her and placed her in God's hands. Right then and there, a huge load lifted off me as I began my journey to listen attentively and esteem her precious.

As time went on, somehow it didn't hurt or sting like it used to. Freed up to love her without putting demands on her, I could be grateful for her no matter what. "The no matter whats" happened at times, and yes, I occasionally slipped into the offense but quickly came out of it by receiving God's grace. Our relationship changed for the better.

At age ninety-eight, as she came to the end of her life, I had something like an epiphany. She was in assisted living. My sister and I expected problems would arise with her strong will, and the staff might make her leave. But the opposite happened! Shockingly, she was so sweet and kind that the staff and nurses loved her deeply. I visited her nightly, and she was a great delight.

She slept a lot and couldn't talk much at the end; yet we were like one, as Forest Gump would say, "Like peas and carrots."[57] By just looking into her eyes, I knew what she was thinking, and those eyes were filled with such love for me. Every night as I sang her favorite gospel songs, she would squeeze my hand, and then open her eyes and grin so big that her eyes seemed to smile too.

I was told she would leave us in a day or two. I cried all the way home. I was so confused; I had to get it out. Upset and wondering why, I protested, "Why did I have to lose her now that she was the mother I had always hoped for? Why couldn't this have happened much earlier to have more time with her?"

The still small voice spoke ever so gently, "I did this for you."

Choking back the tears and anger that had arisen, I asked again, "Why? I don't understand."

What God said next, brought me to my knees. He said something like this: "I wanted you to see your mother as I see her, as if life's experiences hadn't messed her up, as if she hadn't made wrong choices. This is your real mother; minus life's hardships impacting her negatively and minus her brokenness that caused the wrong choices."

Then, I thought about her childhood. It was an excruciatingly difficult one that certainly scarred her deeply. Would I have been the same as her if I had experienced what she did? And what about my mistakes and wrong choices? Were they in part caused by life's hardships messing me up too? That very moment, I felt compassion for Mom, and gratefulness consumed me. I knew that God was healing me from my brokenness (where I had allowed Him to), and He would work on other issues to come.

It was now easy to forgive and pardon every sin and mistake of hers, as God continued to pardon me for mine. I had been given the privilege of seeing my real mother and will always remember her by who she really was and not by what I missed out on.

Graham Cooke had a similar revelation, but said it much better than I did. He taught that the Lord never deals with the old man—it's dead. God always sees the new person in Christ. He does not see what's wrong, only what is missing in us. Cooke gives an example that if I am stressed or anxious, that is the old man, who died in Christ. What is missing is peace, so God will teach me to receive His peace. He doesn't work on the negative—it's gone. He works on giving me the gift of its replacement — peace. [58] Such a good word, Graham!

Put the dead old man back where he belongs in the grave and encourage the new man. Pardon and forgive yourself and others. Forgiveness heals your heart and sets you free. Remember, God always sees you, minus life's experiences messing you up and minus the wrong choices caused by brokenness. He sees you as a new person and encourages that person.

Every situation you find yourself in has a promise with provision attached to it. This time my *Inheritance Promise* was, "Happy are those whose sins are forgiven, whose wrongs are pardoned" (Psalm 32:1, GNT). My *Inheritance Word* was "pardon." When you find out God's will, you can stand on His promise in confidence, no matter what happens.

This fourth promise for you to believe and take as yours is that your sins, faults, and mistakes are under the blood covenant pardon. If you happen to sin, repent; turn from that transgression and receive from God the antidote to the sin, such as peace, faith, love, etc. Complete repentance keeps you free from condemnation and guilt. Now you can pass on the mercy you have received and forgive others. Get back to who you really are in Christ and back under His immeasurable covenant blessings.

CHAPTER 19 – THE ABRAHAMIC COVENANT

5) **The Promise of Provision** [the Inheritance Word]

No longer shall your name be called Abram, but your name shall be Abraham; for I have made you the father of a multitude of nations.

--Genesis 17:5, ESV

In Genesis 17:4, God offered the promise of *provision* to Abram when He changed his name from Abram to Abraham. This wasn't just a name change; it was more like an exchange. God put His name into Abram's name and took on his name.

The Lord's name was Yahwey, Yah for short. The "Y" was silent, leaving "AH." So God put His name *"AH"* right in the middle of Abram (Abr-*AH*-am) which changed the meaning of Abram from "*exalted father*" to Abraham, *"father of multitudes and nations."* [59]

God would make him the chief father of abundant herds, people and nations. He was referred to by God as heir of the world and he had wealth, possessions, and servants. (See Romans 4:13) From then on, God called Himself the God of Abraham.

"As for Sarai your wife, you shall not call her name Sarai, but Sarah shall be her name" (Gen. 17:15, ESV). God put His name, "*AH*," at the end, Sar-*AH*, which changed the meaning of Sarai from "*dominating*" and "*barren*," to Sarah, *"princess* [daughter of the king] *or queen."*[60] Kings would come through them now. Their names were reminders that they were in covenant with God and that He was the source of their provision.

God made them very rich in cattle, gold, silver, and land; even to transferring the wealth of two heathen kings into Abraham's possession. "Abraham fell heir to what others had toiled for" (Psalm 105:44, NIV). He was blessed and empowered by God to prosper in all that he did, so he would be a blessing to others and able to meet their needs. "Abraham was now very old, and the Lord had blessed him in every way" (Genesis 24:1, NIV). They had "the blessing" of God upon them; thus, all their needs were met through this promise of provision.

You too, seed of Abraham, have "The Blessing of Abraham. "But you shall remember the Lord your God, for it is He who gives you power to get wealth, that He may establish His covenant which He swore to your fathers [Abraham, Isaac and Jacob] as it is this day" (Deuteronomy 8:18, NKJV).

And guess what comes with the blessing? "The blessing of the Lord makes one rich, And He adds no sorrow [painful toil] with it" (Proverbs 10:22, NKJV).

Did you see that, heir of God? Wealth is supposed to be sweatless, without struggle and tormenting hard labor. Yes, you are to work diligently, but without depending on your wisdom and skills. It is really about God confirming the blessings of the Abrahamic covenant in your life. The Blessing of Abraham causes amazing things to happen that will astound you. I am proof of this. For example: God sent me to Rome with provision others had toiled for and resources beyond what I could ever have imagined.

Rome

Years ago, God gave me an impression to start praying for nations. I went to my bible study group to ask God which nation we should start praying for. We prayed and waited, wanting

His choice and not ours. What happened next was beyond all expectations. A couple of days later, I got a phone call from a long lost past acquaintance. He had just started a new company for funding nonprofits, and, being Catholic, was going to make a presentation to the Vatican in Rome, Italy. He offered me a position with his company and invited me to go with them, all expenses paid with no strings attached. He thought this would help me decide whether or not to take the job.

Was this a distraction or from God, and why Rome? None of us in bible study were Catholic, nor had we thought of praying for them. As we held it before God, a prophetic word came forth that God would bring me before princes and kings. That sounded great, but now I needed confirmation of God's purpose for me going there other than for business.

God is faithful! I had three confirmations: a prophetic vision, a pastor's words, and a word directly from God. I knew for sure that I was to go there and pray for the Catholic Church, and that I would be given access to strategic places to pray. I wrote down what I was instructed to pray for while there. The contents of the prayers were to be a private matter, so that's all I will say about that.

Determined to be obedient, I packed for the assignment and went to get my hair permed. Wouldn't you know it—of all times, the hairdresser burned the top of my head. My hair started falling out and huge bald spots appeared. What a test for my vanity! At first, I thought about not going, but God convicted me, so I bought a wig. Eat dung, devil!

The first-class plane trip with gourmet food, fine china, and sleeper seats was amazing, along with relaxing in executive lounges on layovers at airports. I was treated like a queen, a blessed queen, I might add. The morning after arriving in Rome, to our surprise, the Vatican gave us a special guide who took us on a private tour of the Sistine Chapel two hours before the Vatican opened. Luigi explained that this was the chapel of the popes. All elections for the Pope were held in this room by the Cardinals.

I knew that Pope John Paul II was weak and would not last much longer. Luigi told the history behind this room and the stories about Michelangelo's artwork. What a place to pray! He then took us throughout the Vatican, even to the basement where the sarcophagi of former popes were.

That night they sent a limousine. Where were they taking us? We had no idea until we pulled up to the U.S. embassy. Jim Nicholson, the U.S. ambassador to the Vatican, was holding a reception for us. We had dinner with him and other dignitaries. He invited us to meet with Vice President Dick Cheney, who was due to be there in a couple of days. We all felt very special indeed. "The Blessing" of the Lord brings favor too among its many benefits!

Next was beyond what we could have ever imagined. The limo took us outside of Rome to Castel Gandolfo on a hill overlooking Rome. It was the Pope's summer residence called the Papal Palace. This was where he entertained presidents and kings. The Blessing of the Lord positions you with princes and kings! I stood alone on his balcony and prayed over Rome.

In the pope's library, I held some of his historical ancient books, and in his observatory, I viewed his grand telescope. Then, if that wasn't enough to thrill us, we were invited to be guests of the Pope that night at his concert called "Reconciliation" and afterwards were to meet privately with him. On Sunday, we went to mass at St. Peters Basilica with the Cardinals.

My little party and I were overwhelmed at the special treatment given us. God in His goodness took us into the very throne room of the Church of Rome. There my prayers were united with all of those throughout the world that have prayed for this troubled church and papacy.

While packing to go home, I glanced out the window to see a beautiful rainbow that started from my hotel with the other end of it right in the middle of the Vatican. What was the significance of this? I had no idea, but took a picture and trusted God to show me the meaning.

At home, I happened to see the Elijahlist. Patricia King had prophesied that God was raising up a company of women intercessors with an assignment to carry the arc of His presence into nations. They would be strategically placed in positions to pray effectively. She added that the Lord would visit many with manifestations of rainbows as a sign that the assignment was fulfilled. This, of course, blessed the socks off me. Thank you, Pat! God is so good!

The memories from this amazing trip would last a lifetime, and though I had the time of my life, I didn't accept the position that was offered to me. I had a check in my spirit (no peace). Sadly, after this, the CEO had a stroke, later died and the company was dissolved. This trip taught me that when God sends, He provides above anything I could have ever imagined. "Let the Lord be magnified who hath pleasure in the prosperity of his servant" (Psalm 35:27, KJV).

Prosperity is not for greed's sake, but for purpose, assignment, and appointment from God. Affluence is for influence. It is purpose-driven for God's glory in fulfilling His plans. And Blessed of God, He will always give you the best because He is glorified in the prosperity of His saints.

The Symbolic Gesture for Provision - A Name Change or Exchange

In a covenant, the initiator would give his name to the recipient. For instance: if Ben Stein made a covenant with Levi

Kahn, he would call his name Ben Kahn Stein. Levi would call his name Levi Stein Kahn. And similar to this, after a wedding, the exchange is announced when the bride and groom are introduced as Mr. and Mrs. "Groom." She carries his name, the source of her provision, and has power of attorney to sign checks, etc. in his name. He is known as the husband of the wife of the covenant.

A name change represented provision through power of attorney. The covenant initiator would say, "My name, and all that it represents is yours. When you sign my name or speak in my name, I will honor it. You represent me, and all my assets and liabilities are yours. I'll always provide for you."

CHAPTER 20 – THE NEW COVENANT

Jesus Continued the New Covenant Promise of Provision

And my God will supply all your needs according to His riches in glory by Christ Jesus.

--Philippians 4:19, NKJV

God offered the promise of *provision* to Abraham through a name change, and Jesus upgraded it big time. The covenant bride of Christ was also promised provision through a name exchange, but this provision was outrageous! Jesus gave His covenant partners not only the use of His name, but the power and authority behind it should they need anything at all. Here's proof of this:

Jesus said, "I tell you the truth, you will ask the Father directly, and he will grant your request because you use my name. You haven't done this before [in the old covenant]. Ask, in my name, [new covenant] and you will receive, and you will have abundant joy" (John 16:23-24, NLT). Did you see it, bride of Christ? When you use the name of Jesus, your request is granted! Really! Take a look at another amazing promise!

"This is the confidence we have in approaching God; that if we ask anything according to his will, he hears us. And if we know that he hears us –whatever we ask – we know that we have what we asked" (1 John 5:14,15, NIV). Wow! This proves how important it is to know God's will in your situation. When you do, you can know for sure that you have what you asked for and boldly ask in faith for Him to do it!

Did you know that Jesus *represented* God, His Father, in everything He did because He always did the will of His Father? In other words, Jesus revealed His Father to others. Jesus said, "Anyone who has seen Me has seen the Father" (John 14:9, NIV). He reflected God's glory by being an exact representation of His nature and being; thus Jesus was like an ambassador. He only said what His Father was saying and only did what He saw His Father doing.

To accomplish this, Jesus had to be given the power, authority, provision, and resources of God so that the Father's will could actually happen on earth, as it is in heaven. Yes, Jesus was God's ambassador, but you, bride of Christ, are Christ's ambassador to bring His will to the earth! Because of the covenant, you became one with Him and are an exact representation of His nature and being. As He is, you are!

"So we are Christ's ambassadors; God is making His appeal through us" (2 Corinthians 5:20, NLT). Now I know you must be wondering, as I did, what exactly does it mean to be His ambassador and what are you to do in this role? Did you know that there are great similarities between God's ambassadors and earthly ambassadors? So, let's first look at traditional diplomats.

USA Ambassador

I know about the role of an ambassador because my uncle, Armin Meyer, was assigned by the President of the United States as U.S. Ambassador to a foreign country called Japan. He was sent there for the purpose of representing the President and American interests. While on assignment in Japan, he was continually protected by the United States Marines.

The ambassador had to be in constant contact with his government to be conformed to the President's will and plans. He could then speak in the name of the President and from his viewpoint. His own personal opinions were not allowed and speaking contrary to the President would constitute treason. This could be reason for dismissal from the position and the provisions it provided.

Armin's residency was the U.S. Embassy, which was selected, owned, and paid for by the American government. Everything he needed to fulfill his position there was supplied by the government. His wealth was not dependent on the economy of the country he lived in, but on that of the USA, his home country. Anyone who entered the gates of the U.S. embassy in Japan was considered on American soil, and they would be under diplomatic immunity and protection from the Marines.

He was a man under the authority of his President; yet, in the land where Armin resided, he was in authority to transact government business and to bring peace there. He carried a position of honor, authority, and royalty. Wherever he traveled, he rode in a limousine that carried the flag and backing of the United States of America.

Ambassador of the Kingdom of God

Can you see the similarities, ambassador of Christ? It's hard not to! You are a diplomat and work for the governmental kingdom of God that Jesus brought to the world. Isaiah spoke prophetically about this. He said that when the Lord would come to earth, He would bring with Him a government. "For unto us a child is born, unto us a son is given: and the government shall be upon his shoulder" (Isaiah 9:6, KJV).

The government and the kingdom are synonymous. You are appointed by Christ to *represent* King Jesus and the governmental kingdom of God. Your kingdom is not of this world but is in heaven. You are a citizen of the kingdom of God, and your homeland is heaven, yet you live in a foreign country called Earth. Your residence, Earth, is where you bring God's government: His will, principles, and precepts. You were sent there for the purpose of *re-presenting* Christ and His interests. While you are on assignment on the earth, warring angels (Marines) are appointed to protect you and yours.

You have access in His name to the same vast infinite heavenly power, authority, resources, and provisions that Jesus had on earth. You can do the same works as He did and greater because of your covenant. As His ambassador, you are the peacemaker bringing peace and healing remedies or cures to troubling events and people. (See Luke 14:31-32; Proverbs 13:17)

You are authorized to speak as His emissary and to speak the Word, what Jesus says. You accomplish this by being in constant contact with Him and His kingdom, to get the mind of Christ and be conformed into His image, will, and plans. You are to speak in His name and from His perspective. If you speak contrary to His will and Word, you may lose the position of ambassador and miss the benefits, provisions, and blessings attached to it.

The home where you live is really God's embassy. Anyone who steps foot on your property is in the kingdom of God and under the diplomatic immunity and protection of warring angels and the laws of heaven. The Lord is your only source, and everything you need is supplied by His governmental kingdom. "And my God will supply every need of yours according to his riches in glory in Christ Jesus." (Philippians 4:19 ESV) Your wealth is not dependent on the volatile economy of the earth where you are assigned but is according to God's riches. Don't miss this. It is according to heaven's riches, not yours! Can heaven go broke? Can it not have what you need? No! God's riches are without limit.

You are under the authority of Christ, but in authority over the things of the earth to transact kingdom business in your sphere of influence. You are royalty and a diplomatic official of the highest rank. Wherever you go, you bring the influence (flag) of the kingdom of God and the backing of heaven is always with you. Never forget, ambassador of Christ, that the source for your provision is Christ and His Kingdom! Seek first and you shall find! I found out more about this quite by accident.

Personal Example of Provision: My Embassy

> The [inheritance] word [provision] will set you up to discover what you're going to experience during the next stage of your journey of faith. [61]
>
> --Graham Cooke

I told you somewhat about this when, several years ago, I lost everything: my marriage, ministry, finances, home, and even my identity. To survive, I moved in with my mother, the last place I wanted to be. To make matters worse, several of my girlfriends were getting their dream homes. I was happy for them, but I felt like an utter failure.

Later, God gave me the perspective that I had lost the past, but not my future. He changed my focus from losing my earthly home to finding my true home, which was at the foot of the cross. I was to seek the King and His kingdom as my only source and know that Jesus would give me a home at the right time. My love relationship with Him was to be my first priority, and as I rested in that love, He began to direct my steps.

Sometime later, I had a defining moment when I read that God had made me His ambassador. (See 2 Corinthians 5:20, ESV). My first thought was that I was a poor representation of God's ambassador. How could I be an example of Jesus when I was divorced, financially bankrupt, in debt, and without prospect of a job or any means of support?

As I pondered my situation, a light turned on. I had an "*aha*" moment. I remembered that an ambassador has to have an embassy. It comes with the territory. Bingo! My faith leapt through the roof as I realized that it was God's will to give me a home, regardless of my circumstances. Then I thought of Paul, who said he was an ambassador in chains to make known the mystery of the kingdom. (See Ephesians 6:19.) If Paul can be an ambassador while in prison, I certainly could be one while in my mother's house. Oh yes! Christ said I am His ambassador; therefore, He would provide the embassy. He said it, I believed it, and that settled it! The revelation of my role as His emissary changed my life.

I acted on this insight by purchasing a red leather chair as a sign of my faith and a point of contact to celebrate my new home before it happened. Believing for my harvest, I sowed what little money I had as seed into the rich soil of a good ministry; thereby, transferring it from the monetary system of my meager finances into God's heavenly system of unlimited supply.

In a very short time, the Lord opened a door. I was offered a job, and I worked hard for almost two years yet had no financial breakthrough. Struggling to make ends meet, I refused to give up but kept the faith by hanging on to God's word: "I am Christ's ambassador." When things appeared hopeless and I wanted to quit, I focused on my red leather chair. Then all of a sudden, my circumstances changed. God gave me favor with some large accounts. I served them, and the money started pouring in.

Two years after buying the chair and planting my seed, it was time to focus on buying my embassy. God had miraculously provided me with the finances to buy my own, but where would that be? For the first time, I knew I wasn't to pick my home. This was God's embassy to be selected, provided, and owned by Him. He would put me where I was needed to bring

His kingdom to others. I only knew that it would be in Orange County, California, so I prayed with my good friend Susan Brooks and waited to hear from God.

The phone rang. Susan had a message for me from God.

"Write these instructions down about your house," she said. "One, it will be by water, two, the price will be $100,000 more than you pre-qualified for and, three, this opportunity is just around the corner." What? How could this be? Homes on the water were way too expensive for my budget, and how could I buy something that I didn't qualify for? And what was up with the "just around the corner thing?"

Nothing made sense. Even though I didn't understand it all, my spirit leapt, and I knew the word was from God. I grabbed it as my own and then it happened. I received a call from my friend, Diane Murray. She had no knowledge of my word from God but knew that I wanted to move. She said, "There is a home for sale that you might be interested in. It's on a lake and it is just around the corner from me." And you guessed it; the home was priced $100,000 over my limit.

I apologized for making such a low-ball offer of $100,000 less than the asking price of the home. It was a peak economy, and houses were quickly selling for full price. Even so, God touched the owner and my offer was accepted. I moved in with $100,000 equity due to the lender's assessed value of the home. And my red leather chair I bought as a memorial of God's faithfulness, looked exquisitely beautiful in my living room.

Later, my neighbors asked me to teach them about God's Word. Soon, three different women's groups were formed and began meeting in my embassy. I believe this all happened because I didn't pursue after money, but trusted in God's covenant provision, the source of all my needs. The Lord had known "the where," "the how," and "the who" of it. He did it all. My part was to just, "Seek first the Kingdom of God and His righteousness, and all these things will be added to you" (Matthew 6:33, NKJV).

You too are His ambassador, honored one! Pursuing the Kingdom of God and Christ's covenant righteousness, as your first priority, brings provision that literally finds you. All your needs are supplied by God, and He will channel the provision through natural means as you are obedient to do His will. Have you been trying to achieve instead of receive, prosperous one? Receive first from God and then achieve.

Every situation you find yourself in has a promise with provision attached to it. This time my *'Inheritance Promises'* were, "We are ambassadors [representatives] for Christ, God making his appeal through us. We implore you on behalf of Christ – be *reconciled* to God" (2 Corinthians 5:20, ESV). The Greek word for "reconciled" means "to exchange lack for His provision; to lay hold of His favor; to exchange your money for His." [62]

Another *Inheritance Promise* of provision was, "But seek first the Kingdom of God and His righteousness, and all these things will be added to you" (Matthew 6:33, NKJV). And my *Inheritance Word* was "provision." God wanted to be my Provider. When you find out God's will, you can stand on His promise in confidence, no matter what happens.

This fifth promise for you to take as yours to believe, receive, confess, and act upon is that God is your source of provision and the only source for all your needs and wants. All He has is yours, and all you have is His. He will supply all your needs. (See Philippians 4:19.) Don't forget that you are Christ's ambassador. Your husband King and His governmental kingdom is the source of provision for all your needs and wants.

CHAPTER 21 – THE ABRAHAMIC COVENANT

6) **The Covenant Promise of Posterity** [the Inheritance Word]

And I will establish my covenant between Me and you and your descendants after you in their generations, for an everlasting covenant, to be God to you and to your descendants after you.

--Genesis 17:7, NKJV

In Genesis 17:7, God offered the covenant *promise of posterity* to Abraham. God asked him to do a very unusual thing: "And you shall be circumcised in the flesh of your foreskins, and it shall be a sign of the covenant between Me and you" (Genesis 17:7, 11, NKJV).

Why in the world would this act be a sign of the covenant; especially since it was a private sign to a person and not to the public? What was God thinking? You probably have wondered about this too. So, let's look at it more closely. This was an irreversible act of circumcision that God chose for the mark of the covenant. Once done, it could never be undone. And it was done by the physical act of cutting off the flesh, which represented putting off the sinful lusts of the flesh and living by the promises of God.

This was personal between God and Abraham's posterity. The Lord made the covenant children the ones who inherit the blessings, not the children of the flesh from natural descent. The uncovenanted were not included in the covenant inheritance. "Any male who fails to be circumcised will be cut off from the covenant family" (Gen. 17:14, NLT).

The circumcision was applied to the organ of procreation (reproduction) to be a reminder to Abraham that his covenant with God was generational. Abraham's children's children would be included in the covenant, until the age of accountability; even those yet unborn.

We have an example of Abraham's great-grandson, Levi, benefiting from this covenant with Abraham. "Even Levi, [the priest] who receives tithes, paid tithes through Abraham, so to speak, for he was still in the loins of his father [Abraham] when Melchizedek met him" (Hebrews 7:9, NKJV).

Levi had not yet been conceived, let alone born, when Melchizedek met with Abraham. The tithe paid by Abraham, however, was attributed to his great-grandson's account. This covenant was permanent, and the blessings applied generationally. This should make you wonder, heir of Abraham, what has been deposited in your account from previous generations. Selah! (Pause and reflect).

A Jew believed that during sexual relations with his wife, the sperm flowed through the circumcision, and that meant his seed was marked for covenant. Don't miss this, son of God, that your children are marked for inherited blessings. That should make your day!

Posterity is important to God. He called Himself not only the God of Abraham, but of Isaac and Jacob. When you said yes to Jesus, you became one with Him in covenant. You entered His lineage that made you Abraham's and David's posterity and heir to all their promises, and so it is with your seed. You can leave a good inheritance to your family and a legacy to the world. It is important to live right, by cutting off the flesh (the lusts) so that these are not the ones passed on to your descendants. The spiritual and material blessings are meant to be continued through your lineage. Here's an example:

David and Goliath

David certainly understood that God is generational, and a covenant is for your posterity. He knew he had covenant rights because he was a descendant in the lineage of Abraham. When the great taunting giant Goliath was threatening the armies of Israel, the Hebrews cowered and trembled at what they saw, but what did David see? He confidently said, "Who is this uncircumcised Philistine that should defy the armies of the Living God?" (1Samuel 17:26 KJV).

OK, why would David call Goliath "*uncircumcised*"? Had Goliath's pants fallen down? No, David didn't need to see that part of the giant. He knew Goliath served other gods, and that meant he could not be in covenant with the living God or receive the promised inheritances. This "*un-covenanted*" *giant* was no match for one who was in covenant with God and an heir of Abraham.

David was young, a mere seventeen-year-old boy, yet he was confident in the faithfulness of a covenant-keeping God. What could have made him so bold? Perhaps he knew that as the posterity of Abraham, he had the covenant right of protection.

David said, "The Lord that delivered me out of the paw of the lion and out of the paw of the bear, he will deliver me out of the hand of this [un-covenanted] Philistine" (1 Samuel 17:37, KJV). David didn't look at the size of the giant, but at the size of the covenant he had with God.

By faith, David saw the giant from Gath as a defeated foe and saw himself standing on top of the giant collecting the conquerors reward. He not only told this to Saul, the king of Israel, but spoke it to Goliath, the enemy of Israel. He made a declaration, "This day the LORD will deliver you into my hand, and I will strike you and take your head from you" (1 Samuel 17:46, NKJV). He proclaimed the covenant promise and of course God gave him the victory. Being confident in the Lord's faithfulness, David slew the giant effortlessly and cut off his head.

The Israelite army could have defeated the giant since they had the same covenant as David, but instead of faith in God, they feared. Unbelief and fear prevented God from moving on their behalf, until a young boy who could see through the eyes of faith appeared. The image David had in his mind of defeating the giant became a visible reality for everyone to see. Who could doubt it was God? Faith rose up in the army of Israel when the Philistine army ran away, so they pursued after them and finished them off.

David took Goliath's head to Jerusalem and buried it on a hill. The hill was later named Golgatha, "the place of the skull"— "Gol" from Gol-iath and "gath" from the city he was from. This was prophetic because many years later, Jesus, of the lineage of Abraham and King David, would be crucified on this same hill. The cross was in the same place as the buried skull of Goliath. David defeated the enemy of Israel (Goliath), and here on the cross, Jesus defeated the enemy of all mankind, (the devil), by cutting off his head of power as had been prophesied in the Garden of Eden. God said to the devil, "He [Jesus] will crush your head, and you [devil] will strike his heel" (Genesis 3:15, NIV).

When you said yes to Jesus, you became one with Him in covenant and entered His lineage. You are Abraham's and David's posterity and heir to all their promises. You can say to your evil enemies, "Who is this un-covenanted demon? You are under my feet and tremble at Christ in me."

The Symbolic Gesture for Posterity – A Memorial or Token

The initiator of a covenant always gave a memorial of something that symbolized posterity. This was to be a constant reminder of the longevity of the covenant throughout generations. It might have been a flock of sheep that kept reproducing, trees planted, a heap of stones, a scar, a ring, or, in Abraham's case, circumcision. If the covenant was ever broken, the covenant breaker and the family would have to die, because he and his descendants were now under the curse. As you can see, this was all about being faithful to the covenant for generations to come.

CHAPTER 22 – THE NEW COVENANT

Jesus Continued the New Covenant Promise for Posterity

In other words, it is not the children by physical descent who are God's children, but it is the children of the promise who are regarded as Abraham's offspring [posterity.]

--Romans 9:8, NIV

The covenant God gave to Abraham was between him and his descendants after him forever, and it was marked by circumcision. Jesus took circumcision from the physical organ of procreation and upgraded it to be a circumcision of the heart, the organ which is the source of spiritual life. Oh yeah! Now women can get in on the circumcision. Your heart is the production center of your life. "Watch over your heart with all diligence for from it flow the springs of life" (Proverbs 4:23, NASB).

Jesus brought circumcision from outward actions to the inward motives of the heart. It went from the physical to the spiritual, from the law and man's abilities to God's abilities and what He could do in and through man. Paul wrote, "But a Jew is one inwardly, and circumcision is a matter of the heart, by the Spirit, not by the letter" (Romans 2:29, ESV).

The Mosaic law of the old covenant was about rules: "Thou shalt not murder" and "Thou shalt not commit adultery." You could have a heart full of hate and want to kill or a heart full of lust, but as long as you didn't act on these, you were innocent of murder or adultery. People were judged by the outward appearance.

Jesus made circumcision a spiritual matter of the heart and no longer about a code of behavior or set of rules and keeping the laws. It was about the condition of one's heart. He said, "But I say to you that whoever looks at a woman to lust for her has already committed adultery with her in his heart" (Matthew 5: 28, NKJV). And John added, "Whoever hates his brother is a murderer" (1 John 3:15, NKJV). There was now a big difference between the law, with its rules to keep, and the motives of the heart. Check this out. This may be a new perspective for you.

A *law*yer [an expert of the old covenant law] came to test Jesus by asking Him, "Which is the greatest commandment in the law?" (Matt. 22:36 KJB) There were over six hundred laws to be kept at that time. Jesus answered the question by quoting the old covenant law instead of sharing about the new covenant of grace: "Thou shalt love the Lord thy God with all thy heart and with all thy soul and with all thy mind and the second is, thou shall love thy neighbor as thyself. On these two commandments hang all the law and the prophets" (Matt.22: 37-40, KJV). The stage was set; the lawyer had asked Jesus about the law of Moses, and Jesus answered about this old covenant law which was to love with all your heart.

True Love

Now this law sounds good and right and is a worthy goal we all should attain to, but my question to you is this: how's that working for you? Can you consistently keep this law? Are you able to love God with all your heart, where nothing comes between you and Him--nothing like anger, blame, fear, busyness, or anything that upstages that love? Have you ever had ugly neighbors or obnoxious people who think and act differently than you? Do you love them to the same degree that you love yourself and bless those who curse you?

The law is impossible to keep, isn't it? Even the Bible tells you that. I know that your goal is to love God with all of your heart and your neighbor as yourself. It's the best objective to have. I have that goal too, but how do you get there? Do you try harder? Pray more? Study more? Worship more?

I knew I was deficient in that kind of love, so I asked the Lord, "How can I love You more?" His response surprised me. I heard in my spirit, "You can love Me [God] because I first loved you" (see 1 John 4:19, NKJV). Then I saw it! "First" comes before "second." I was to be loved by God first, and after that, I would be able to love with all my heart. Did you notice this was not the old law, but the new covenant? This revelation took me from performance of trying to love, to just receiving His love. I had to get filled with His love, saturated in it, and then let it overflow to others.

John, the apostle of love, gives the definition of love: "This is love, not that we loved God, but that he loved us" (1 John 4:10, NIV). This was about God doing it through you, loved of God. No more struggle or guilt! The new covenant of grace was about relationship from the heart and was different from the old covenant order. John got this. He referred to himself as "the one Jesus loves," not the one who loves the Lord. None of the other eleven disciples seemed to get this, yet we know that God was no respecter of persons and loved them all equally. John understood and declared it (five times) with boldness because he was consumed in perfect love.

When John was with the mother of Jesus at the cross, Peter was away weeping. Peter had depended on *his* love for God, even boasting that everyone else might desert Jesus, but he never would. I believe he really thought he could love that much. After denying Jesus three times, the realization hit him hard that the love he had for Jesus was not enough. John, however, knew that God's love was always enough and joined Mary at the cross in the midst of serious persecution. Then an interesting thing took place that caused me to wonder.

Mary had other children that would take care of her when Jesus died; yet Jesus chose John for this responsibility. "When Jesus saw his mother there, and the disciple who he loved standing nearby, he said to her, 'Woman, here is your son,' and to the disciple, 'Here is your mother.' From that time on, this disciple took her into his home" (John 19:26, 27, NIV).

OK, so now you have to wonder, why were the brothers and sisters of Jesus not chosen? Could it be that John, the apostle of love, could pass on, not his love for her, but God's love for Jesus's mother? Hmmm! Food for thought.

I was once like a lawyer interested in keeping the law and trying hard to please God. But isn't the law based on works and performance? Didn't Jesus come to shift us from the law to grace? Isn't Jesus our Source, who does everything in us, through us, and for us and we simply receive it? The heart of the New Covenant is just that. He initiates, you receive, and then you love others with His love.

Are you confused at times with one foot in old Mosaic Law and one foot in the new covenant of grace? All the old covenant laws of "Thou shalt or shalt not" Jesus later summed up in one law of love. He said, "A new commandment I give to you, that you love one another, *as I have loved you*" (John 13:34, NKJV). Oh, did you see it, loved of God? "Love one another" is present tense, and "as I have loved you" is past tense. Now that is important! God was saying in essence, "Come into My presence and enjoy being loved. When you have been loved by Me, you can love others from My overflow." He didn't say, "Love one another with all your heart."

To be able to receive His love, you need a new nature. Human nature, since Adam, was sinful and focused on self-realization and man's abilities without God. That was the old man. Christ went to the source of the behavior and "circumcised" the heart by cutting away your sinful nature. "When you came to Christ, you were 'circumcised,' but not by a physical procedure. Christ performed a spiritual circumcision—the cutting away of your sinful nature" (Colossians 2:11, NLT).

When Jesus took your sins on Himself, He gave you His righteous nature in exchange for your sinful nature. Righteousness vindicated you from sin. This was life changing! Don't miss this, saint. You are a totally new person. He removed the Adamic nature to make you a new creation in Christ, born from above. As a new man with a new nature of righteousness, you have a choice to follow the old man, which is your fleshly lusts, or to respond to the love of God.

Your heart can not be fully satisfied until it finds out who it was made for. God loves with a love no one can match, and by being full of His love, you can fall in love. His love shows you how special and valued you are and who God made you to be. After this recognition, you are able to love God, yourself, and others to that same degree. Masaru Emoto said, "To love yourself is to love and thank all of existence."

God's faultless love, filling your heart, makes it possible to love even the unlovely. Jesus says, "Love your enemies, do good to them which hate you, bless them that curse you, and pray for them which spitefully use you. Do unto others as you would have them do unto you" (Luke 6:27, 28, 31, NKJV).

An awakening to love was at hand. This awakening was about the restoration of love, resonating in unity with Jesus Christ, who was the personification of perfect love. This circumcision of love and blessing was to be generational. It was the Lord who would do the circumcising, not only to your heart, but to those of your children. The love of God would be passed on to your posterity. That saint, ought to put a zip in your step!

This was prophesied about what Jesus would do in the new covenant. "The Lord your God will circumcise your hearts, *and the hearts of your descendants*, so that you may love Him with all your heart, and with all your soul, and live" (Deuteronomy 30:6, NIV). Without Jesus doing the spiritual circumcising (the cutting away of your sinful nature), your love is impure, inept, and incomplete.

God is generational and has separated the posterity of Abraham and its blessings from the children of the flesh. But no worry, heir of God, those in covenant with Jesus Christ are the seed of Abraham and the Lord's inheritance.

All creation is groaning and waiting for you and your posterity to take their rightful place. As the sons of God emerge in the power of pure love, the creation will recognize and respond to that sound. Could this mean the world will know we are Christians by our love because our love is His love? I think so. Don't you? The following is an event that revealed to me more about the promise of posterity.

Personal Example of the Covenant of Posterity: A Miscarriage

> The [inheritance] word [posterity] will set you up to discover what you're going to experience during the next stage of your journey of faith. [63]
>
> --Graham Cooke

Years ago, I had begged God to save my daughter's baby and my posterity. Heidi was miscarrying at three months. The placenta around the baby had come out. That meant it was a hopeless situation, because without it, the child would surely die.

I tried to muster up faith in the midst of my panic, when God's voice interrupted my requests to save this child. He said,

"What about Me?" Then He reminded me of His Word, saying, "Children are a heritage of the Lord and the fruit of the womb is My reward." (See Psalm 127:3)

At first, I thought, *what do you mean, what about Me?* Then I saw it. Satan was trying to steal God's glory, to kill generations because every baby is God's reward. The focus wasn't to be about Heidi and me or our pain and desires. Instead of begging for my will, this was about finding His will and surrendering to it. God wanted agreement from me for what He desired to do, so that He could step into this situation, together with me, and bring about His successful outcome.

I got on my face and repented for not making it about Him and for not looking for His will and plan. At that moment, the fire of God's presence came on me. Immediately, I was caught up in a vision. I saw three types of women. I knew one was my pregnant miscarrying daughter, another was the pregnant church—but she had no strength to birth (See Isaiah 37:3)—and the third was America who was barren.

I saw that the land of America had been covenanted with Jesus Christ by our founding fathers and was richly blessed until her leaders no longer wanted God's plans for America. They kept pushing Him out; therefore, she was becoming barren and unfruitful. The enemy had moved in to steal the heritage of our forefathers and the heritage of God Himself.

Then God spoke again, "Do you agree that all three are hopeless, unless I breathe on them?"

I responded, "Yes, for sure!"

He continued on, "Watch what I do to your daughter, it is what I will also do to the church and America at the appointed time."

Wow! At that very moment, I knew God was going to breathe

on Heidi's womb to resurrect and restore life to my granddaughter's heart (my posterity; His heritage). That sounded beyond wonderful but why would He do this? I knew that it wasn't due to my begging. Then I saw it. This was because we were all in covenant with Him; my daughter and me, the church and America. We were His heritage!

Unshakable faith rose up in me because now I knew God's will was to thwart Satan from killing my posterity and stealing His glory. I came into agreement with Him. My voice became His voice, as I authoritatively decreed that Satan could not steal God's glory. This baby would live! In unwavering confidence, I called my daughter, "You are about to see a miracle."

The doctor made sure again that there was no placenta and that the baby was dead. Since she hadn't come out of the womb on her own, he arranged to suction her out. Before allowing that procedure, Heidi made the doctor do another ultrasound and monitor the infant's heart again, but her hope was shattered. There was no placenta around her and no heartbeat. The baby was lifeless. As the doctor turned around to begin preparations, suddenly a sound came over the heart monitor, *Tha-thump*; then another, *Tha-thump*! And another!

The baby had come alive! To the shock of everyone, the ultrasound showed a perfect placenta restored around her. God had breathed life into Heidi's womb, and she birthed a miracle. Brianna Nicole was born six months later, an exceedingly strong and healthy baby girl.

And it didn't end there. Another miracle happened twenty-four years after the miraculous birth of my granddaughter (God always uses twenty-four to confirm serious things with me). To everyone's surprise, Donald Trump won the presidency. It was called a miracle, as all odds were against him. His goal was to make America great again, which he did, and it was the best economy ever. But more importantly, he brought us back to a "nation under God." God's original intent for our nation was to be the greatest voice of the gospel. Here's what this president said, "Faith is more powerful than government and NOTHING is more powerful than God." [64] (President Trump –Trending Politics)

Within his first term, he brought worship and prayer meetings back into the White House, defended prayer in schools, gave protection for the faith-based organizations, brought Jesus back in Christmas and promoted pro-life. As top leader of the land, he proclaimed Jesus Christ as Lord. Could this be God breathing on America's barren womb? Could this be the time that God will breathe on His church and strengthen her so she can birth and usher in the third great awakening? This is a definite possibility, don't you think?

Every situation you find yourself in has a promise with provision attached to it. This time my '*Inheritance Promises*' were, "Children are a heritage of the LORD: and the fruit of the womb is His reward" (Psalm 127:3, KJV). God had promised, "Watch what I do to your daughter, it is what I will also do to the church and America at the appointed time." My '*Inheritance Word*' was "posterity." When you find out God's will, you can stand on His promise in confidence, no matter how impossible the situation may be.

This sixth covenant promise for you to take as yours—to know, believe and receive, act upon and expect—is that God will circumcise your heart as well as the hearts of your descendants because your seed is marked for covenant. This covenant is generational! You were known by God before you were conceived, and He has a purpose and a destiny for you and your children. Spend intimate time with Him. Say, "I am loved of God and have received His love, so I am able to love. He has circumcised my heart and those of my children to love God, myself, and others. My seed is marked for the covenant blessings because of the blood covenant." Don't ever stop praying for the salvation and blessings of your children!

CHAPTER 23 – THE ABRAHAMIC COVENANT

7) **The Covenant Promise of Perpetuity** [the Inheritance Word]

By Myself have I sworn, saith the Lord: that in blessing I will bless thee, and in multiplying I will multiply thy seed as the stars of heaven, and as the sand which is upon the sea shore.

--Genesis 22:16-17, KJV

In Genesis 22, the Lord swears an oath to Abraham, a pledge of perpetual blessings and multiplication of his seed that would never end from generation to generation. God would personally uphold His word of the promises. They would come to pass and could never be revoked because God alone carried the responsibility of keeping them. "Heaven and earth will pass away but my words shall not pass away" (Luke 21:33 KJV).

"By Myself have I sworn, saith the Lord." There is no one greater than God, so He swore by His holiness, faithfulness, and truth. "For when God made a promise to Abraham, because He could swear by no one greater, He swore by Himself" (Hebrews 6:13-17, NKJV). That means, saint, God can't do anything unsacred or disloyal to His word, nor can He lie. You can bank on that.

To protect these promises, God released Abraham from the responsibility of keeping the covenant. By doing this, there would be no chance for Abraham to break the oath and cause a curse to come upon his future generations. Oh yeah! That meant that perpetual blessings to Abraham's descendants would never ever end. And heir of Abraham, that affects you and me!

When God pledges, you can expect that what He says will come to pass:

> My covenant will I not break, nor alter the thing that is gone out of my lips. Once have I sworn by my holiness that I will not lie unto David. His [David's] seed shall endure forever and his throne as the sun before me. It shall be established forever as the moon and as a faithful witness in heaven.
>
> --Psalm 89:34-37, KJV

God swore with an oath on His own holy character, where He brought the universe into the pledge regarding the continued existence of the solar system. As long as the sun and moon kept their appointed places, they were witnesses that God would not stop David's descendants, and Abraham's, from being royally blessed. "If my covenant be not with day and night and if I have not appointed the ordinances of heaven and earth; then will I cast away the seed of Jacob, and David my servant so that I will not take any of his seed to be rulers over the seed of Abraham, Isaac, and Jacob" (Jeremiah 33:25-26, KJB).

As long as you see the sun and the moon, you are assured of His promises. God is a Covenant Keeping God; a Promise Keeper. And since you are the seed of Abraham, Isaac, Jacob, David, and Jesus, you are blessed of God unto perpetuity. That is part of your new identity. The Blessing of God is on you, and you live under the blessings of Abraham and David! It's your birthright!

The Power of an Oath – David and Jonathan (1Samuel 18)

The Bible gives us an example of a godly eternal covenant made between David and Jonathan unto perpetuity. Jonathan, the son of King Saul and heir to the throne, deeply admired David when he was a mere shepherd boy. Jonathan made a covenant with him because he loved David as himself.

To do this, Jonathan took off his robe and gave it to David, along with weapons of war, such as his armor, sword, bow, and belt. They *swore* to one another that this covenant would last between them and their descendants forever. Neither had any children yet, but they knew a covenant was generational and perpetual. David understood keeping the *oath* and the longevity of an eternal covenant. He knew that if the oath was kept, God would bless them, but if it was broken, curses followed.

Jonathan's father, Saul, was a very insecure king. Feeling threatened, tormented, and jealous of David's popularity and abilities, the king tried unsuccessfully to kill David, forcing him to flee for his life. Sadly, David never saw Jonathan again, but always remembered their covenant union.

Nine years later, David was sorely grieved over the news that King Saul and Jonathan were killed in a battle. After their deaths, the relatives of the house of Saul panicked, not knowing about the covenant of blessing between Jonathan and David. "If David ever became king," they reasoned, "he would return the evil that Saul did to David and kill us." Fearing for their lives, they prepared to hide out.

While fleeing in terror, the nursemaid to Jonathan's five-year-old son, Mephibosheth, accidentally dropped him. He became lame in both legs, never to walk again. Lodebar, a rebel outpost in the dry desert, was the place chosen for Saul's relatives to hide away. It was here they would plot to fight against David if need be, but as the years passed by, all of Saul's descendants were killed in wars. Mephibosheth was the only family member remaining.

After David was made king of Israel, he remembered his covenant oath made with Jonathan twenty years before. King David inquired about Jonathan's children, "Is there yet any that is left of the house of Saul that I may shew him kindness for Jonathan's sake?" (2 Samuel 9:1, KJV). He was told about sixteen-year-old Mephibosheth hiding in Lodebar.

The King immediately sent chariots, and they surrounded the camp. Poor Mephibosheth. Unkempt and living in poverty, he thought his life was over as they quickly whisked him off to the palace. Trembling before King David, he collapsed and begged for his life, "Have mercy on me, my lord."

He cringed in anticipation of the reply. But he heard something that made no sense. Had his ears played tricks on him? Instead of anger, David spoke to him with great love and tenderness. He wanted to bless Mephibosheth with lands, money, and possessions. The king wanted his presence at his table daily as his adopted son. How could this be?

"*I, I'm not worthy,*" Mephibosheth stuttered. *If you only knew,* he thought, as his mind reflected back on the times he had spoken against David. In shame, he whispered quietly to himself, "*I am a dead dog.*" But David had not made the offer on the basis of Mephibosheth's merit but on the blood covenant oath he had made with his father, Jonathan.

The covenant with Jonathan would stand from generation to generation. It didn't matter that Mephibosheth had plotted against David or that his grandfather, Saul, had tried to kill David. What mattered was the covenant! It brought Mephibosheth into the family of the king as an adopted son.

Mephibosheth now had life changing decisions to make--to live in a hut or in a palace, to live in rags or in riches, to be a servant or a son, to be unknown and hidden away or to have a royal position in the kingdom. If he accepted the offer, he must separate himself from David's enemies and live in loyalty to the king—and sit at the king's table. He would now have to choose between the blessing and curses. How could he not accept this magnificent offer?

Mephibosheth's ignorance of his covenant rights and benefits had cost him big time. He was living way beneath what was available to him until David sent for him. So, I ask you, does a covenant benefit you if you don't know what belongs to you? Absolutely not! The benefits are available and accessible but not automatic. You have to believe they exist and take hold of these blessings.

Whatever you need is available through the blood covenant. Now God says to you, "Is there anyone of the house of Jesus Christ, whom I can bless?" Your part is to say, "Yes! Here I am." In doing so, there is a divine reversal. You walk in a peasant and walk out royalty. By inheriting the kingdom of God, you begin to live in the riches and royal position of the King. It is your new identity!

The Gibeonites

About four hundred years earlier, there was another perpetual covenant made that was not based on love, like was David and Jonathan's. Even so, it was still unbreakable. This one was between Joshua and his enemies, the Gibeonites. The Gibeonites were enemies of God and Israel. Fearing destruction by the Hebrews, they decided to trick Joshua and his men. Though they lived nearby, the men of Gibeon deceitfully pretended to be ambassadors from a faraway place and came to make covenant with Joshua. Lying even more, they told of hearing about the God of Israel and wanted to serve Him and Israel.

Joshua and his men unfortunately made covenant with them without inquiring of the Lord. They swore to the Gibeonites to keep peace and protect them from their enemies forever unto perpetuity. Without knowing it, they had sworn to protect the enemy of Israel and the enemy's enemies. What a huge mistake this was! All of it was based on fraud, deceit, lies, and betrayal. *Oy vey!* You would think that when Joshua and his men realized the deception, they would make the Gibeonites pay with their lives. But oh no, that didn't happen! What transpired next was mind-blowing.

When Joshua discovered they were Gibeonites, the enemies of Israel, he said this:

> We have sworn unto them by the Lord God of Israel; now therefore we may not touch them. This we will do to them; We will let them live, lest the wrath of God be upon us because of the oath we swore unto them. However, they were cursed because of their lies, but allowed to live as servants and bondmen.
>
> --Josh 9:19, 20, NKJV

Later, five kings gathered together and encamped around the Gibeonites to kill them. The men of Gibeon panicked and sent word to Joshua to honor the oath and come quickly to save them. Now God entered the scene, and this part was almost unbelievable. The Lord slew the enemies of Gibeon with a great slaughter by casting huge stones upon them. As if that wasn't enough, when the sun started to go down and the battle had not been fully won, Joshua asked God to make the sun stand still. They needed more time to defeat these five kings and their armies. I bet you didn't know that the sun stood still so that Israel could save Israel's enemies, who were in covenant with them through deceit. Wow! This was ridiculously absurd.

You see, when a covenant was made with an oath sworn before God, that brings the Lord into the equation as part of the covenant. Did you realize that if you break your covenant, you are actuality breaking covenant with Almighty God? He was obliged by the law to send curses upon the covenant breakers, and Joshua knew this.

Now get this. It doesn't end here. About 450 years later, King Saul of Israel killed some of the Gibeonites, who would have been their enemies had Joshua not covenanted with them hundreds of years earlier. Because Saul had broken covenant with the Gibeonites, God sent a famine on Israel for three years. Remember a covenant is perpetual! David knew better. When he became king, David inquired of the Lord, why the famine? The Lord answered, "It is for Saul and for his bloody house, because he slew the Gibeonites" (2 Samuel 21:1, KJV). God had to forever protect the Gibeonites (Israel's enemies) because of this prior covenant.

David immediately called for the men of Gibeon, asking what could be done to atone for the covenant Saul had broken so that the Gibeonites would bless Israel. Since Saul was already dead, they wanted Saul's brothers, sons, and grandsons to be killed. David obliged and killed them all except Jonathan's son, Mephibosheth. Killing him would be breaking David's covenant with Jonathan. Did you really see this, heir of God? A covenant is never ever to be broken unto perpetuity. This is serious stuff! Wouldn't you agree?

The Symbolic Gesture for Perpetuity - The Swearing with an Oath

When the covenant initiator and recipient would swear with an oath, they would swear before God. That was serious business because if the oath was kept, blessings would overtake them, but if broken, curses would pursue them.

"All these blessings shall come upon you and overtake you, because you obey the voice of the LORD your God" (Deuteronomy 28:2, NKJV). "All these curses will come upon you. They will pursue you and overtake you until you are destroyed because you did not obey the LORD your God" (Deuteronomy 28:45, NIV).

God had sworn with an oath to bless those who obeyed Him, but He knew the Israelites would break covenant. God can't bless sin, so He created a plan where He could bless them again. If they obeyed by offering animal sacrifices yearly on an altar to atone for their sin, God would forgive them for that year.

Because of these blood sacrifices, they were blessed, not on their own merit, but because the sacrifice atoned for their sins. (See Exodus 20:24) The covenant initiator would swear with an oath and say something like this, "I swear an oath before God to keep this covenant as long as I live unto perpetuity. I will never betray it or neglect it. I will give my life (which Jesus did) to maintain the integrity of this bond."

Of course, this was just a harbinger of what was to come. God had a future plan to redeem them from their sins and forgive them not for a year but unto perpetuity through the sacrifice of His own Son. Oh, how God loves to bless His children!

CHAPTER 24 – THE NEW COVENANT

Jesus continued the New Covenant Promises with the Pledge of Perpetual Blessings

His mercy extends to those who fear him, from generation to generation, to Abraham and his descendants forever, just as he promised our ancestors.

--Luke 1:50, 55, NIV

The Lord swore an oath to Abraham, a pledge of perpetual blessings and multiplication of his seed that would never end. After the Law of Moses was introduced, curses resulted if Israel disobeyed God. Jesus upgraded this promise. In the new covenant, the curses were changed into blessings. Jesus rescued His followers from any curses when He hung on the cross. The crown of thorns, and the cross, were both products of the curse and there for a reason. Jesus took upon Himself the curse that comes from wrongdoing and sin. "Christ has redeemed us from the curse of the law being made a curse for us" (Galatians 3:13, KJV).

The kingdom of darkness and death still exists today but has no legal right to rule over God's children who are in covenant with Christ. We have been redeemed from these curses. The kingdom of darkness will still aggressively oppose God's Kingdom of Light. The violent [furious believer] doesn't tolerate evil, but is intentional to rule over it, seizing the bounty that rightfully belongs to them. (See Matthew 12:28.) You win by the force called faith, faith in the Covenant Keeper and His word of promise. You now inherit the covenant blessings and not the curses. Is this great or what?

The blessing is God's love in manifestation for eternity (perpetuity). It involves salvation, health, wisdom, revelation, light, grace, mercy, favor, glory, joy, and righteousness, to name a few. "But this Man, after He had offered one sacrifice for sins forever [unto perpetuity], sat down at the right hand of God, For by one offering He has perfected forever [perpetuity] those who are being sanctified" (Hebrews 10:12,14, NKJV).

Saint of God, you are perpetually made righteous, and a causeless curse can't light on one blessed of God. The new covenant brought together earth's material blessings and heaven's spiritual blessings. The most powerful force on earth is "The Blessing." It distinguishes you from all others.

What does this all mean? When you fail, fall or sin, there are consequences, but no curse unless you agree with darkness. Jesus did away with generational curses. Now you are not to swear with an oath because if broken, you get curses. Here's the biblical proof:

> Again, you have heard that it was said to the people of long ago, 'Do not break your oath, but fulfill to the Lord the vows you have made.' But I tell you, do not swear an oath at all: either by heaven, for it is God's throne; or by earth, for it is his footstool; or by Jerusalem, for it is the city of the Great King. And do not swear by your head, for you cannot make even one hair white or black. All you need to say is simply 'Yes' or 'No'; anything beyond this comes from the evil one.
>
> --Matthew 5:33-37, NIV

Did you get this, blessed of God? Never swear with an oath!

No more do sins need to be passed on to the third and fourth generations. You have the legal right and authority to stop the sins or curses by agreeing and partnering with Jesus, the Word of God. You've been rescued from spiritual death, poverty, sickness, and disease into the abundant life of blessings that Jesus gave you unto perpetuity.

God has given everyone a choice. "I [God] have set before you life and death, the blessing and the curse. So, choose life in order that you may live, you and your descendants" (Deuteronomy 30:19, NASB). Agree with God's promise of eternal life and blessing. The choice is entirely up to you, but you must act on it. Here's an example:

Personal Example of the Promise of Perpetuity: Dad's Salvation

> The [inheritance] word [perpetuity] will set you up to discover what you're going to experience during the next stage of your journey of faith. [65]
>
> --Graham Cooke

Dad was an atheist and an alcoholic. I knew that God wanted him saved and it was time to prove the power of the perpetual blood covenant's inheritance promises. I found the promise in Joshua 2:13, where God saved Rahab's house when she asked, "Promise me that you will save my father and mother" (Joshua 2:13, GNT). I also stood on Acts 16:31 (ESV). It says, "Believe in the Lord Jesus, and, you will be saved, you and *your household*." I continually prayed for my father, reminding God that I am His covenant child and believe His word. I asked Him not to let my Dad die until he had met Jesus.

Nothing changed for quite some time, but that did not deter me from believing God's word. Later, I received a shocking phone call. In a somber voice, my father told me that his doctor discovered cancer in his lungs, the result of prolonged smoking. The prognosis was terminal. He feared death, yet continued to reject the Giver of life. Darkness overtook him with night sweats of torment and fears that constantly awakened him during the night. Still, he refused to hear about Jesus.

A few months later, he was admitted to the hospital and lapsed into a coma. Doctors said he would never wake up. I reminded God of my covenant inheritance promises as I sat daily by his bedside. One day upon entering his room, I noticed he was alone, something which was very unusual. Suddenly his eyes opened. He searched the room and then looked directly at me.

"I am going home tomorrow, Lornah," he clearly stated.

"Uh, what do you mean by that, Dad?" I inquired. I thought he was delusional. I assumed he meant going home to his house.

What I heard next was bittersweet. He said, "Jesus appeared to me and invited me to come home to heaven with Him. I asked Him if I could stay here on earth a little longer, now that I know about Him, but He said, 'No' - so – tomorrow I am going to heaven."

Fighting back the tears, I asked if he was afraid to die to which he responded, "Oh no! Not at all, but I wish I would have known what you have known all these years." God in His goodness had gifted me with this time alone with my father. He reassured me that my prayers were answered and that someday, I would see my dad again in heaven because he had eternal life with God.

The expected call came early in the morning; however, the call that followed was mind-boggling. My dad's atheist friend and drinking buddy dropped dead of a heart attack the same day that my father died. While I was trying to make sense of it, the Lord spoke to my spirit. I heard, "He didn't have anyone praying for him. He is going to hell. Don't ever think your prayers are unimportant."

Wow! This proved the seriousness of believing God's covenant promises and praying them in faith. It can be a matter of life or death, heaven or hell. My dad is in heaven's eternity and we will meet again on the other side.

Did you realize, child of God, that your prayers are this important? They can change a difficult situation into God's intended purpose. Every situation you find yourself in has a promise with provision attached to it. This time my '*Inheritance Promise*' was, "Believe in the Lord Jesus, and you will be saved, you and your household" (Acts 16:31, ESV). And my '*Inheritance Word*' was "perpetuity." When you find out God's will, you can stand on His promise in confidence, no matter what happens.

The seventh promise for you to take as yours, to believe, to receive, confess and act upon is that God pledged and swore with an oath that His words and promises are perpetual. Say, "I believe I have received all the rights, benefits, blessings and promises of God that are everlasting and unending. I choose life and blessing that will be passed on to my seed forever. I am eternally blessed of the Lord because of the blood covenant."

Heir of God, you have been given great and mighty riches of the Kingdom through your blood covenant with Jesus Christ. Always remember your seven inheritance words:

1) A *partnership* with the Trinity
2) God's *protection* and your authority over evil
3) A *position* as heir of the family and kingdom of God, and heir of Abraham
4) A *pardon* from all sin and failures
5) *Provision* for your needs and desires, so you can bless others.

6) This includes your *posterity* (descendants).

7) Unto *perpetuity* are all the blessings of God.

These will drastically change your life. You will never be the same!

CHAPTER 25 – SUMMARY OF THE SEVEN PROMISED INHERITANCES

My Story

Have you ever lost everything, all at once, including your identity? As you know, years ago, in what seemed like a moment, my life drastically changed when I plunged into a dark abyss and groped to find some solace amid the multitude of my losses. It was the adulterous betrayals and the loss of my twenty-four-year marriage that pierced my heart the deepest. My dreams died with it that would forever lie unborn in a grave.

My home was foreclosed on, and all finances and income gone. My ministry was over, perhaps forever, or so I thought. There, in the midst of great uncertainties, I stood by myself, grief stricken and left alone to pick up the shattered pieces. I somehow lost me. No longer the wife of my husband, who was I, and what would become of me?

It fell heavy on me--cold and foreboding like a chilling dense fog obstructing the light of the midnight moon. The sounds of hisses and jeers could be heard in the darkness of my despair. The sinister thief, who came to steal, kill, and destroy, was howling in celebration of my fall. I was shattered, heartbroken and alone. I wept until I could weep no more.

Initially my prayers were filled with sorrowful cries like a loyal German shepherd despairing over the demise of his master. Fear overtook my emotions and confusion grabbed hold of me, turning me upside down. I felt much like a fish out of water. Intense loneliness enveloped me that first night in the tiny bedroom of my mother's house that was now my home.

All of my clothes were thrown over pieces of her furniture, hanging there out of place as they testified to my pitiful condition. This was the last place on earth I wanted to be, especially at my age. It felt like I had failed at life itself.

I poured out my hopeless condition to the Lord, reminding Him repeatedly that I had lost everything, as if He didn't know or care. Pitying myself in the injustice of my circumstances, I was inconsolable at first... until I heard that voice.

It was a mere whisper, yet so powerful that it penetrated the torrents of tears and spoke hope to my spirit. Clearly and convincingly God said, "You have only lost the past, and now you have a new beginning." It was His amazing love, not sympathy, which pierced the darkness of my soul so that shame and despair could no longer stay in His presence. His words were so commanding that I believed Him and fell asleep worshiping the One who cared for me. Later, I would find out that God used this very difficult circumstance to give me the seven promised blessings of Abraham.

Knowing my need, the Lord began to show me from His word what He wanted to do for me in this situation; what He wanted me to inherit. My inheritance promises were, "He raises the poor from the dust and lifts the beggar from the ash heap, To set them among princes, even the princes of his people, And makes them inherit the throne of glory. He makes the barren woman, to keep house, and to be a joyful mother of children" (1 Samuel 2:8; Psalms 113:7-9, NKJV).

Did you notice God's part, child of promise? He "raises," "lifts," "sets" and "makes it happen." He does it all. Wow! Perhaps you are wondering why God would do that for me. It's because I am in covenant with Him, that's why! These scriptures were now my promised inheritances. Oh, glory be! *In Christ* all my needs would be met. I knew God's will for me in this particular situation of betrayal and divorce. I was to believe His Word and pray with passion as He and I joined together to see these promises come to pass. There was life after betrayal!

Within a very few years, I could look back and see that all of these verses had been fulfilled. And guess what? The seven promised inheritances given to Abraham were included within these very scriptures. God is so good, amazing and profound!

By separating out each inheritance promise, I will explain what God did in my situation and how He did it, to encourage you because God's word is for you too. "For all the promises of God in Him are Yes, and in Him Amen, to the glory of God through us" (2 Corinthians 1:20, NKJV).

The Promise of Pardon

1) *He raises the poor from the dust.*

1 Samuel 2:8, NKJV

In Biblical times, dust usually represented shame, guilt, worthlessness and humiliation.

Here is an example:

King David experienced an excruciatingly shameful time of betrayal. His own son, Absalom, sought secretly to take the kingdom away from his father and kill him. David got wind of it, so he and his men fled from Absalom. Along the way, Shimei, a man from the house of Saul, rode beside him cursing and throwing stones and dust at David. This was an act to shame him publicly.

Shimei shouted for all to hear, accusing David of being a

bloody, evil, worthless good-for-nothing man of the devil, and that God had taken his kingdom and given it into the hand of Absalom (See 2 Samuel 16: 5-14). Now that wasn't true, but I wondered what must have been going on in David's mind and heart at that time? Was he hurting from the sting of betrayal and questioning his own integrity?

I could relate with the pain and humiliation. Divorce has a stigma with it. People sometimes point fingers and judge you without knowing what went on; thus, for a short season, I carried a load of guilt, hurting deeply, and questioning my very worth. Betrayal from anyone is hurtful, but from a loved one, it can be one of the most agonizingly painful things you can go through. Then if you add guilt and shame to the betrayal, it goes way beyond hurt to torment. Pastor Robert Morris said, "Guilt and shame takes out more people than sin."

Like David, I needed God to raise me up. I was down for the count. I wanted to be set free from guilt, shame and betrayal. As I felt His mercy, goodness, and consuming love, I broke and repented for missing out on opportunities to connect with Him and to find His agenda. I received God's pardon and then forgave myself. When I did, He began to take me on a treasure hunt in the darkness. There, He planted secret riches to discover profound things about Him and beautiful things about myself that I never knew before.

In a judicial system, a pardon releases the prisoner to a whole new life of freedom and liberty. God says it better in His word, "Freedom is what we have—Christ has set us free! Stand, then as free people, and do not allow yourselves to become slaves again" (Galatians 5:1, GNT).

To be set free, I must reckon the emotional, old self dead and buried and not be held captive by what man thinks of me. (see Romans 6:11, NKJV.) This was my opportunity to live free in the resurrected new man of God, going from a bondman (victim of my flesh and other's wrongs) to a freeman. God wanted to deliver me in a very difficult situation. The harder the circumstance was, the greater the rewards would be! In other words, stand fast in the resurrected new free man, and don't go back to the old man of victimization, guilt, and shame--he's dead.

I wasn't to focus any longer on the wrongs of sin or mistakes, but on the important things, like losing God and His intense love for me during this hardship. When I lost God, I lost me and my identity of who God says I am. I had to ask myself these questions: who was I really? Was I not enough, or more than enough in Christ? Was I a victim of circumstances, or a child of God, highly favored and deeply valued? In my weakness, did I still have authority over the demonic realm and the things of the earth?

By repenting and receiving God's pardon in the middle of this, my conscience was clear. I could start seeing my real identity in Christ. At the right time, God raised me above shame and guilt to show me who I really was in Christ--a new creation. I could now walk with confidence in who God was making me to be, regardless of the situation. Eventually, I could confront the betrayal, not from a position of anger, fear and weakness, but from strength.

I had to forgive my husband and stop shaming him by trying to make him feel guilty. That never works! It is only a temporary fix. He will eventually resent the one shaming him. This was my chance to be conformed into the image of Christ, "Father forgive them for they know not what they do." (Luke 23:34)

It took a while, but as I experienced God's love, mercy, and grace, I began to extend forgiveness until I was able to give a full pardon. Pardoning others sets you free from any residue from the past and forgiving yourself frees you from guilt and condemnation. My hope and expectation for a great future grew and blossomed into one. Yes, God did raise me out of the dust of shame and set me free!

The Promise of Provision

> 2) The promise continues on: "*He lifts the beggar* [desolate, destitute, in lack] *from the ash heap* [garbage dump, dunghill]." [66]
>
> --1 Samuel 2:8, NKJV

After losing everything, dread came upon me at the thought of looking for a job. It felt like more loss. How could I start over? For eighteen years, I was in ministry, which was on the shelf for now; thus, I had no resume that would warrant a good secular job. Some said, "Flip burgers if you have to." The pressure from others to find work at any kind of job, regardless of what it paid, became another weight to bear until I heard the Lord's sweet voice. He said: "You don't need any more loss, how about you do something that feels like gain to you?"

Gain? I hadn't even come close to thinking about gaining. My thoughts were continually on how much loss I had to bear, but God did get my attention. I wondered what gain would look like for me; certainly not a job at that time. Then college came to my mind. I thought about what it would be like to go back there. First, I questioned how I could pay for it without income. Then I thought about my age compared to the young students. That might be awkward and uncomfortable; however, I would be learning new things. Ah yes, learning would be gain to me. I love to learn! With that, peace overtook me as a smile broke through my dismal countenance. God is brilliant!

The first day at school, I learned about grants. I was eligible for free money. Yahoo! They would pay me to go to school! I took classes like business, computers, advertising, and anything that related to jobs.

When it was time to get a job, I was ready. I visited friends who "*just happened*" to have a dinner party to go to that night. They invited me and I "*just happened*" to sit next to a gentleman who owned a company, and during our conversation, he felt led to ask me to go to work for him. Yay God!

I knew this was a divine set up, so I accepted commission only. After the first year of working really hard, I barely made any money. I was confused, somewhat disillusioned and thought of quitting, but felt led to hang in there for another year. I'm so glad I did! My boss asked me to sell his new product, dry wall shims, for the construction industry. I asked, "What's a dry wall shim?"

He said, "I really don't know much about it. You'll need to figure that out."

And figure it out I did, with some heavenly help. I thought that I might as well go after the large accounts, as they take the same effort as getting the small ones. I knew all odds were against me, because we were a small unknown company competing with the big boys. For the big accounts to change their vendors, it usually took payola or a bribe, and that wasn't possible for me. I knew, however, that in Christ, all odds were for me. God hadn't brought me this far to end in failure. He loves to shine in hopeless situations and bring opportunities out of impossibilities.

It was obvious that God gave me favor. In a short time, I landed three huge accounts, one with over two thousand stores. Overnight, my income went well into six figures, and it was residual income. From then on, every time an order came in, I received a check. My company nicknamed me the "Queen of Shims," and I felt like a queen. Now I had more free time and could pursue my passion—writing and teaching. God had lifted me out of the dung heap of poverty, providing way above my expectations.

The Promise of Position

3) *To set them among princes, even the princes of his people.*

--1 Samuel 2:8, NKJV

God opened doors to set me with some princes of His people. Not when I had it all together, mind you, but while I was unknown and hidden away in obscurity in my mother's little bedroom. My life was in transition; yet the Lord saw to it that I sit with men and women of destiny. I never sought after, nor desired this prince part, but God was faithful to *all* of His word.

This was not about my qualifications, but about who God says that I am. I was nameless, neither a CEO of a Fortune 500 company nor a pastor, but still God chose me to sit with pastors and kings. I was a king in training, like David hidden away in the cave. I was trained, not in a classroom, but tucked away in a little bedroom. Isn't that just like God?

Rick and Kay Warren

God brought me before princes in a way I never expected. It was time for me to get new single friends as most of my friends were married. I had heard that Saddleback (Rick Warren's church) had a great program for singles. Feeling uneasy and awkward, I went there by myself. It was a huge service of about fifteen hundred singles. Talk about intimidating!

Afterwards, we were invited to fellowship at the nearby food court. Being shy and not knowing anyone, I headed for home. Just then, I had a strong impression to turn around, so I went back. Among the many tables, there was only one seat available. I sat down and found everyone to be so very friendly, especially Jim, the guy next to me.

During our conversation, I told him that he had an uncanny resemblance to Rick Warren, to which he replied, "I hear that a lot." He invited me to church functions, and we became close friends, along with several women that I met there. Later on, Jim told me that he was Jim Warren, Rick's older brother, but people called him, "the Prince."

I learned much from the teachings of Rick and Kay Warren. I had the honor of sweet fellowship in their home, gleaning from who they were, and how they live their lives. They were the real deal! In addition, I was blessed with three wonderful years with Jim "the Prince," until unexpectedly one night; he passed on in his sleep. These memories and the impact each person had on me will last beyond a lifetime. Thank you, Lord, for these divine appointments! You really did set me with the princes of your people.

God connected me with several more princes, but the point I wanted to make was this: God made it happen. Did you notice that? He directed the show. He was the potter, I was the clay. There was no struggle or toil, just a lot of stretching and enlarging my borders. God works on the inner man, cherished of God. He brings hidden riches from secret places. He will position the least likely with princes, even the princes of His people. God is faithful to His word!

The Promise of Partnership

> 4) *And makes them inherit* [take possession, occupy] *the throne* [seat of honor and authority] *of glory.* [67]
>
> --1 Samuel 2:8, NKJV

Because of the covenant, you share the throne of authority in the kingdom of God in *partnership* with your King. "And [God] raised us up together, and made us sit together in heavenly places in Christ Jesus" (Ephesians 2:6, NKJV). The queen was to sit beside her King. Why? It was because in a marriage covenant betrothal, the two have become one. It was to be a shared life. The bride-queen or son of God was a non-gendered thing, and both males and females were to be the recipients of the covenant. This was not based on performance but on the covenant partnership with the Godhead. This partnership was your inheritance!

Dr. Myles and Ruth Munroe

To teach me more about this covenant union, God introduced me to the mysteries of the kingdom of God through the teachings of Dr. Myles Munroe. You can't inherit what you don't know. Ignorance is not bliss! Here's how God did it:

One day when I was walking by the TV, I heard Dr. Munroe's voice. His words caught my attention as he shared the kingdom of God in a way I had never heard before. My spirit leapt. Who was this man? I wanted to know more.

God's familiar voice spoke to me, "I want you to go to him and sit under his teachings." That sounded good to me! I ran to the computer. His church was called the Diplomat Center, a place where leaders are trained. A conference was scheduled there in two weeks, and get this, it was in the Bahamas! Oh yeah, God! I always wanted to go there.

At first, I was thrilled to be going to Nassau, but the excitement lessened as foreboding fearful thoughts hit me like, *This isn't God. You will be going out of the country all alone, to a strange place, not knowing anyone. You don't even know anything about this man. This is crazy, you can't go. It's too expensive.* Fighting those fears, I booked a non-refundable flight right then and there, so I wouldn't get cold feet and back out later.

The travel preparations came together easily with what seemed like God's fingerprints all over it. The first night of the conference, I sat in the back of nearly a thousand people. I couldn't wait to hear Dr. Myles' words of life. Unfortunately, someone else was speaking, whose words fell to the floor without much meaning. At the end of the evening, no one talked to me, and I felt all alone and confused. Had I missed God? Had I blown it and wasted my money. Should I go home? I tossed and turned all night.

Early that morning, as the sun peaked through my drapes, I heard the most enchanting sound coming from my balcony. I opened the slider, and there sat two beautiful white doves on the railing. These lovebirds didn't scatter but sat there, looking right at me and cooing as if serenading me. Oh my! *Was this from God,* I wondered?

I dressed and went down to breakfast. I needed to talk with someone and the waiter was a willing ear. After I told him about the beautiful doves that seemed very tame, he shook his head. "Oh no, mon!" he explained. "You could not have seen doves. They don't come here this time of the year." He was adamant that not a single dove was on the island. My heart skipped a beat as I felt the kiss from my King.

With my hope restored, I went eagerly to the conference. This time I sat in the very front row. Again by divine choice, I "just happened" to sit next to Dr. Lucile Richards, the executive director of the International Leadership Training Institute located there. She invited me to her home for lunch, and soon we became very close friends. Dr. Myles spoke during the rest of the conference, and he was amazing. His teachings exploded within me, and I received much more than I expected. Not only was I learning about the kingdom of God, but I began seeing the covenant from a kingdom perspective. The prior revelations that I had about the covenants took on a whole new meaning.

I jumped at the personal invitation to come back later with a special group of less than forty people. We were locked away in a hotel for three days with Dr. Myles, from early morning to late at night, but it seemed only a few hours. I was in heaven. I had come to the Bahamas like a lamb, but I left like a lion—bold and confident. Rrrroar! Another kiss from my King!

I went back to the Bahamas (the place where God lives, Myles says) for three more conferences. And whenever he and his wife Ruth came to Los Angeles or Orange County California to speak, I had the privilege of spending time with them. God is so good!

I believe God used Dr. Myles to show me the glorious splendor of the kingdom and the partnership from the throne, so that I would be able to share the covenant partnership with you from a kingdom perspective. And did you notice that God instigated all of it. He *made* me inherit the throne of glory, the seat of honor and authority.

Jesus doesn't choose the qualified, but qualifies the chosen. And don't worry, God has a sense of humor. If He chose me, a divorcee, to be given revelation on the covenant marriage, there is hope for us all! That is because He loves to use the foolish to confound the wise. Ha! You have been chosen. Enjoy your partnership on the throne of His glory and get used to wearing a crown.

The Promise of Perpetuity

> 5) He [God] maketh the barren woman…
>
> --Psalm 113:9, KJV

The word *"maketh"* can mean "*marries*" and *"barren"* means *"childless, unfruitful, desolate."* [68] This says that God marries the barren desolate woman. It is not when she has it all together, but when she needs to depend on Him. This is a marriage covenant with Jesus that can never be broken. It is *perpetual.* Jesus, as your eternal spiritual husband, brings forth spiritual children through you, as He conforms you into His image.

After my divorce, I felt alone, desolate and useless—barren if you will. Then I had an amazing encounter with God. When I was trying to figure out single life, my Lord spoke to me. He said, "Read Isaiah 54. It is the kingdom for the bride of Christ, (the covenant recipient)."

Isaiah 54

> Sing O barren, You who have not borne! Break forth into singing, and cry aloud, You who have not labored with child! For more are the children of the desolate than the children of the married woman. For your Maker is your husband, The LORD of hosts is His name; And your Redeemer is the Holy One of Israel; He is called the God of the whole earth. For the mountains shall depart And the hills be removed, But My kindness shall not depart from you, nor shall My covenant of peace [favor, prosperity, health, safety, security, welfare, and happiness] be removed. [69]
>
> --Isaiah 54:1, 5, 10, NKJV

This scripture tells you that God uses the desolate barren ones to birth His purpose. Perhaps that is why there were several women in the Bible that were barren. Sarah, Rebekah, Rachael, Hannah, and Elizabeth were barren, yet all of them ended up birthing children of promise. Sarah birthed Isaac (see Gen. 11:30; 21:2). Isaac's wife, Rebekah, birthed Jacob (see Gen. 25:21,24). And Jacob's wife, Rachel, birthed Joseph (see Gen. 30:1, 23). Hannah, birthed Samuel the prophet (see 1 Sam. 1:5, 20). And Zechariah's wife, Elizabeth, birthed John the Baptist (see Luke 1:7,57).

It was out of barrenness that fruitfulness came. That's because God intervened, breathed upon their wombs, and they all birthed, "the heir and child of promise." The purposes of God were fulfilled. Take a look at the story about Hannah. I think you will find it interesting.

Hannah

When Elkanah's wife, Hannah, was barren, his other wife, Peninnah, had many children. Hannah was grieved by it, perhaps because she felt she had disappointed her husband. But that was not the case. Elkanah said to her, "Am I not better to you than ten sons?" It was evident that he loved Hannah. She received double portions from him. This tells me that Hannah was most likely the covenant wife, while Peninnah was more like a concubine.

Now the point I want you to get is this: it was the covenant wife, not the concubine, who birthed the child of destiny (the purpose of God) and got the inheritances. The names of Pininnah's children, though many, were not even mentioned!

Hannah means *"favored of God."* She was chosen of God, and when He opened Hannah's womb, she birthed God's purpose; Samuel, the prophet of God. Hannah celebrated the birth of her son, but it is what she sang that tells it all. She confidently stated, "The barren [Hannah] hath born seven; [Seven – means the destined one] and she [Pininnah] that hath many children is waxed feeble." (1 Sam. 2:5, KJV).

The name of Hannah's husband Elkanah means, *"God has taken possession."* And betrothed one, when your husband, Jesus Christ, has full possession of you, you too will birth His eternal promises during desolate difficult times. This is His promise to you! Start singing in the midst of troubled times. Your Maker is your covenant husband unto perpetuity! He will bring good out of it. I know because I experienced a certain situation where my Maker revealed Himself as my faithful husband. He took me from despair to delight during a very challenging time.

My Experience – Mom's Car

When my husband went belly up financially, the house was foreclosed on. The day before the foreclosure, he left, leaving me alone to fend for myself. "Scared" took on a whole new meaning, and I felt so very much alone. What was I to do? Where was I to go? Not knowing what to do, I called my mother and was relieved that she invited me to come home. While packing, somehow I lost my car keys and had to leave my car there. I rode in the moving van to her house.

After that dark night with torrents of tears and being consumed in my losses, I told God something like this: "Lord, you have to be my husband now more than ever. I don't have a husband to take care of me." I really needed to know that He was with me in this difficult time.

That next morning, I drove my mother's car to the dealership so they could make a new key for my car. As I drove down the off ramp from the freeway, her car made a horrible sound, violently jerked, and came to an abrupt stop. My heart sank as I surveyed the situation. I couldn't believe my eyes. The axle had broken, and the front wheels had fallen out sideways. A desperate feeling came over me. Have you ever felt like when it rains, it pours?

The sudden awareness of not having a husband to call grasped hold of me. A few tears began to form as I wondered, *"Where are you, Lord? You're supposed to help me. What else can go wrong?"* There was only silence as I tried to gather my thoughts. I left Mom's car on the side of the road and walked to the dealer. They made the key for my car, but I had no way to get to it, so I asked if they could drive me there. The answer was a sharp, "No! It's too far and against policy."

That did it! Unstoppable tears streamed down my face like a burst dam. Embarrassed, I took off running, but had no place to hide. I ran into the restroom and entered the commode stall. Falling on my knees, I cried out, "Where are you, God! I thought you were my husband." What I heard next was earth shattering.

The voice said, "I just saved your life, and no mortal husband could have done that for you."

Wait, what? Confused I repeated His words, "You just saved my life?" Then I saw it. I had gone seventy plus MPH on the freeway, and the axle didn't break at that high speed. Instead, it broke at the end of the off ramp when the car was going very slow.

These tears were different. I felt God's love and how much He cared for me. A heart full of gratitude rose up within me, "You're so right. Only you could have saved my life." Somehow, I didn't feel alone anymore. I knew it would be OK. God would work it out. I washed my face and left the restroom. The service manager was anxiously waiting for me to come out. He nervously apologized, "I will take you to get your car, wherever it is." Smiling, I thanked him, but first I needed to call a tow truck to pick up my mom's car.

As the car was being hoisted up on the truck, the driver glanced at the freeway, then back where the car had sat. His expression changed. His next words made me grin really big. He said, "OMG, you had just come off the freeway, right?" I nodded, yes. He continued, "If the axle would have broken then, at those speeds, well let's just say, it wouldn't be a pretty picture. I've picked up the pieces when this has happened to others. You must have someone up there looking after you."

Boy, did he get that right! "Yes sir, that I did; it was my husband, Jesus Christ."

God always remembers covenant. It's eternal, perpetual, forever; in other words, loved of God, it will never end! The Lord is your perpetual husband and will always take excellent care of you. He has your back. He's got you covered, whether you are single or married. This is really about the promise of His faithfulness to the covenant, and getting a successful outcome from every desolate, troubling situation you find yourself in. God loves to shine!

The Promise of Protection

6) *"[He makes the barren woman], to keep house,"*

--Psalm 113:9, KJV

A home is considered to be a sanctuary. It is a refuge, a place of peace, safety, and security for a woman; to a guy, it's his castle. That tiny bedroom in my mother's house, where I was residing was neither *my* bedroom nor *my* home. That's why it felt strange to me that first night. The bed was unfamiliar, the night unusually dark and foreboding. I felt so out of place, insecure and all alone but in the middle of that night, I had a dream.

In it, I was with a lot of my friends bicycling. We were having a great time, laughing and enjoying riding through my neighborhood. Suddenly out of nowhere, ominous clouds appeared and thunder and lightning went off in the distance. I knew I needed to get all of us back to my house for safety. They eagerly followed me as I turned into my cul-de-sac, but my home wasn't there. What was happening? Was I on the wrong street?

We turned around and went to the next one, but that wasn't it either. They continued following me from one cul-de-sac to the next to no avail. The storm had hit hard and we were drenched, cold, and scared. I was desperate by then. Why couldn't I find my home? At that moment, I woke up in an agitated state, and looked around in the dark but didn't know where I was—nothing was familiar. Then I remembered. *Oh!* I was at my mother's home. I sighed, "No wonder I can't find my home. I don't have one."

God in His mercy helped me deal with this loss. He asked me to take my focus off my loss of not having a home and to make my home at the foot of the cross. I trusted Him as I learned to be content wherever I was. God would be my home and my refuge in a storm, my ever-present help in trouble. And like King David, I was to bring it down to one thing, "This only do I seek; that I may dwell in the house of the LORD all the days of my life, to gaze on the beauty of the LORD and to seek him in his temple" (Psalm 27:4, NIV).

It was His presence and protection I was to seek. As I did, everything else began to seem pale in comparison to the beauty of the Lord. And you know how the story goes; later, the Lord did give me a beautiful home to keep, way beyond my wildest dreams. It was my embassy from God on the serenity of a lake filled with the sounds of ducks, geese, and a few swans in the day. Then at night, the reflection of multicolored lights danced over the water as if they were celebrating God. It was a heavenly home where I was safe and secure!

The Lord had chosen the perfect place for me to reflect on His beauty, so I could write about Him and discover more of who He had made me to be. Seeking the Lord pays rich dividends. All you have need of will find you. "But seek first the kingdom of God and His righteousness, and all these things shall be added [increased, put together for a purpose] to you" [70] (Matthew 6:33, NKJV). Did you notice it says, "things" will be seen? So, protected one, put His house first and it will become your protection, safety, and refuge from all the storms of your life. Then enjoy the home He will or has given you!

The Promise of Posterity

7)[The barren woman is]to be a joyful mother of children.

--Psalm 113:9, KJV

God loves to turn barrenness into spiritual fruitfulness. Since children are the heritage of the Lord, God births His child of promise (the promised word fulfilled) through you, especially where you are a victim of circumstances that has made you desolate and barren. And did you notice He will give you, not just one child, but many. And these children of promise will give you exceeding joy.

As you know, the hardest situation I have encountered was betrayal. Why is an adulterous betrayal so difficult? It is because betrayal is cruelty to another, and when done to you, it is hard to bear and excruciatingly painful. It makes the future seem hopeless, divorce imminent, and your dreams dead and buried. Adultery is a broken covenant that has inconsistencies of lies and deceptions that cast a net to destroy the innocent. It diminishes the wife in her own eyes to wonder who she is, and if her best isn't enough, where does she go from here?

But glory to God! He loves to step in and open the womb of the desolate, to birth His promises and purposes right in the midst of devastation. These children are not birthed by your flesh, lusts, or desires, but by God's pleasure. It's all about you and Him connecting, so that together you birth the promised inheritances.

In childbirth, the labor pains can be intense. God doesn't cause hurt, but uses painful situations so you can know Jesus in the fellowship of His suffering. "That I may know Him and the power [miraculous strength] of His resurrection, and the fellowship [shared partnership] of His sufferings, being conformed to His death" (Philippians 3:10, NKJV).

By dying to the old fleshly man that wants things like vengeance or retribution, you can instead reckon yourself dead to those sins, but alive to Christ. Now as the "new man," you will birth, not the results of your sin, but your destiny in the power of His resurrection. Have you thought on this, child of destiny, that exceeding great joy comes out of sorrow, and that for a resurrection to happen, there must be a death? Kent Christmas says, "You can't reign with Christ if you can't suffer with Him." [71] Let me explain. A good example is Leah.

Leah – Genesis 29 –

During my situation of betrayal, I appealed to God, "What are you doing in this? And what is my part? Father, this feels so cruel and unjust, yet I know that you are never cruel; not ever, nor do you allow cruel injustices to overtake me."

I waited and heard something surprising from God. He didn't answer my questions, but asked me a question. He said, "Oh really? What about Leah? Was that a cruel situation?"

My thoughts went to her. I recalled how Leah had struggled year after year in a loveless marriage. She had to watch her husband, Jacob, love her beautiful sister Rachel. Suddenly I could identify. My heart began to hurt for her, and I blurted out, "Oh yes, that was cruel! It wasn't even her fault. She was innocent. Lord, why did you let her go through such cruel agony?"

The impression came to me to go back and read the process that Leah went through and find the outcome. As I did, I read that when God saw that Leah was unloved by Jacob, He opened her womb. She was no longer barren and became so fruitful that she popped out kids like a vending machine. Leah named her first child Reuben, because she said, "The Lord has noticed my misery and now my husband will love me" (Genesis 29:32, NLT) But he still didn't love her, so she birthed another son hoping that would do it.

She called him Simeon, "Because the Lord heard that I was unloved, He gave me this one too" (Genesis 29:33, NET). Becoming even more desperate, she named the third baby, Levi, who became the priestly line. "Now this time will my husband be joined to me because I have born him three sons," she said in Genesis 29:34 (KJB).

Poor Leah. Even though she gave Jacob a good posterity, it was not enough to win Jacob's love. Most likely, she felt "less than," that she wasn't enough. As the years of cruel agony continued on, she grew weary. Her name meant *"weary,"* and Leah lived up to that name. [72] Everything appeared hopeless and cruel until something began to change. No, it wasn't the situation that was altered. It was her that changed.

While stuck in the middle of this cruel unfair situation, Leah birthed Judah (Judah means "praise," "to be grateful," "a marriage song of celebration") [73]). "This time I will praise the Lord," she joyfully declared over her forth son (Genesis 29:35, NIV). All right! Did you see it? She was praising God *"now,"* no matter what was going on in her life.

The desperate victimized Leah died when she stopped trying to get Jacob's love and turned instead to being grateful and praising God. Leah found God in the midst of affliction and birthed God's purpose. Through Judah's lineage came King David, whose kingly blood line birthed Christ, the Lion of Judah. Oh yeah! Now can you see it? She transitioned from "loss" to "life," from death to resurrection.

But what about Rachel? Her name meant, *"soft, dubious, shady."* [74] She was beautiful in her outward appearance that caused Jacob to be instantly attracted to her, but what about the inner beauty? She stole her father's images [gods] and then lied to him about them. Jacob, not knowing what Rachael had done, decreed that whosoever had stolen them, let them not live. Later, Rachel died in childbirth.

After Rachel's passing, Leah spent many more years with Jacob. She became a woman of character, a woman who served God, not idols. I think her inner beauty made her outwardly beautiful also. I believe Jacob fell deeply in love with her. Why do I think this? It's because Jacob buried Leah, not Rachael, where he would be: in the family tomb along with his parents, Isaac and Rebekah, and grandparents, Abraham and Sarah. Now that says a whole lot. Don't you agree?

Leah was changed on the inside as she went from trying to do better, or trying to control difficult situations and people, to trusting God and praising Him. She went from death of a relationship to love resurrected and to God's successful outcome.

Can God be cruel? No, he can't. He is always working to bring great good out of cruel situations. Some might say that if He allows it, that's cruel. I don't agree. Cruelty comes from human beings, not God. He gives mankind a free will, which is free choice, and God will not violate that choice. Wrong decisions may be hurtful and cruel, but God always has a plan in it. He waits for you to agree with what He, not you, wants to do in the situation. Only then can God reveal Himself and call you up to a new level in Christ.

God has plans for you that will knock your socks off. Bill Johnson gives an awesome revelation on this: "The situation that appears to destroy your life is the platform for a great promotion."[75] Together, the Lord and you in covenant are enough to handle any situation. Joyful one, could the Lord be calling you to birth "praise" in the midst of cruel troubles? Think on that!

The Lord promised these seven amazing promises of blessings, benefits, resources, and privileges to Abraham, and if you are in Christ, they belong to you also. You are promised partnership, protection, position, pardon, and provision to you and your posterity unto perpetuity. These are your *Inheritance Words*. In any situation you encounter, look for God's word that is His will for it, and stand on the *Inheritance Promise*.

Life is not about you or me. It's about God within, teaching us to live according to His will that influences others in the way of the Lord. Every journey you are on, has a silver lining; great good that comes out of it. Since that's the case, lamb-hearted lion, choose wisely, and find God's will in it. Focus on the win and have each journey turn into a great celebration! Keep looking up, highly favored and loved of God! God believes in you and so do I! Until we meet again…

EPILOGUE 1

Song of Innocence

Sometime after my divorce, I went back to school at a community college. One of my classes was a writing class where the instructor asked us to write about our lives and tell our story. I chose to use the prose from Song of Solomon because I could identify with the Shulamite, and I called it, "Song of Innocence." I had no idea the instructor would require me to read it to the class. It was something so private and personal that I really didn't want to read it, especially in a secular school. I stumbled through it, and when I finished, you could hear a pin drop--dead silence.

Finally, in the awkwardness of the moment, a guy asked, "Was that about God?" To which I replied, "Yes, it was." Then a young woman burst into tears and ran to me. Falling into my arms she told me that she used to be a Christian but was really backslidden. With that, the teacher abruptly dismissed the class. The guys dashed for the door, obviously very much relieved. Then several women surrounded me to tell their stories of regret and how they wanted to change their lives. This beautiful experience was a divine appointment after all. I hope you enjoy my story.

Song of Innocence

"She has no breasts," the young boys snickered. I didn't exactly hear them say it, but I knew what they were thinking about me. My older sister was the object of their affection, being well endowed at an early age. The contrast to her was sharp, like putting a pine board next to an intricately carved cedar chest.

Perhaps I could buy a bra and stuff it, but would that suffice? I wanted to be desirable too.

As I grew, my breasts developed and overflowed with cleavage, and my thighs curved like smoothly carved pillars. The boys no longer thought me undesirable. But why did I? It seemed not enough to just look like a woman. I was empty on the inside, perhaps from the jeers of my alcoholic father or the neglect of an absentee mother, and feeling like half a woman, though my exterior would not give me away. Was this hypocrisy, appearing outwardly attractive yet inwardly alone and afraid, a mere child in need? Had adolescence played a cruel trick on me?

I was dark, but lovely. I was made to keep others vineyards but my own I did not keep. Looking to others to define who I was, I tried to please the suitors that came eagerly to court me. Garnished on the outside, my building was overlaid with precious gems and glittering gold. The boys whispered words I longed to hear of their love and devotion for me. "*I am enraptured by your beauty,*" they proclaimed. "*You are the only one for me.*" Their eloquent words caressed my ears and increased my expectations, until they were found sneaking off to be with another.

Taking advantage of my neediness, they trampled my tender shoots in pursuit of selfish gratification and shut up my fragrant spices of myrrh and aloes. Stripping off my veil of innocence, they wounded and bruised my pleasant fruits and left me alone to pick up the pieces. Am I only an object to be played with or a painted building with no foundation?

Tattered and torn from betrayals, lies, and deceptions, such was the fate of this victim. My garden lay waste in ruins, walled and boarded up with spikes that dripped with blood, violated by my own wrong choices. Bound by the cords of their betrayals, my constant companions became insecurity, distrust, and disappointment.

Is life just a facade and do knights exist only in the minds of young childish Cinderellas? Is there a slipper that can make my feet dance and spin like a top in unbridled abandonment? Would I ever be a princess, whole, with nothing broken, nothing missing? Somewhere beyond the haze of darkness and confusion there must be truth that would set me free.

By night on my bed, I sought the One I would love. I sought Him but did not find Him. "*I will arise now,*" I said, "*and go about the city; in the streets and in the squares to find the One who loves me.*" Scarcely had time passed when I found Him. I held Him and would not let Him go.

He was not a mere mortal man but was the embodiment of all goodness and love. He was the Way, the Truth, and the Life. Like an apple tree among the fir trees was my Beloved among men. I sat down in His shade with great delight. Because of my fear of the night, He encompassed me with angels, valiant men expert in war, all holding swords. Chiefest among ten thousand was my Beloved, my Friend.

He awakened me saying, "*Rise up from discouragement and come away with me.*" His eyes were aflame with passion. "*You have ravished my heart with one look.*" Blowing upon my garden with words of life, He kept calling to me, "*You are the fairest among women, fair as the moon, clear as the sun and awesome as a conquering army. You are all together fair with no spot in you.*"

Oh, but would He find me out when morning came and see the darkness hidden in my soul? "*Don't look upon me,*" I quietly whispered, "*because I am dark.*" Not listening to any of that, He repeated again and again words of restoration. It mattered not to Him that I had imperfections and weaknesses. Mistakes and blunders are kissed away by His mercy and grace.

Never varying in his faithfulness, He spoke and caressed my wounded soul. When I saw myself as a lily of the valley, sort of a common variety among thousands, He quickly refuted it. "*You are much more,*" He declared. "*You are a lily among thorns; the finest filly among the king's chariots; as beautiful and lovely as the finest capital cities. You are the perfect one, the only one among sixty queens, eighty concubines, and virgins without number.*"

I was in the eye of the beholder and altogether lovely. I was the apple of His eye. I was my Beloved's, and His desire was toward me. My good added nothing to it, and my bad took nothing away from it. Some may judge me according to who I was, instead of who I was becoming, but His judgment was righteous. He saw my end from the beginning and knew my innermost thoughts.

He kept blowing upon my garden reminding me of whose I was until fruitfulness overtook the desolation. Before I was even aware, my vines had flourished; my pomegranates budded, and my soul had made me as the chariots of nobility. When others devalued me, I stood as a wall, my stature like a palm tree: straight, tall, and protected. "*I am a wall and my breasts are like towers. I am fully woman; not just a body, but a spirit and soul.*" (see Songs 8:10)

My own vineyard is before me now, priceless and equal to His. Having now my own identity, I was no longer barren. I had been redeemed coming out of the wilderness like pillars of smoke, perfumed with myrrh and frankincense. I had broken forth into singing. He had made me to know who I really was: the undefiled, the fairest of women, not merely a princess but a queen espoused to the King, the One who holds the key to my heart and the destinies of men in the palms of His hands.

The daughters now wait to hear my voice and desire to follow in the path where I have gone because my path leads to Him. I love Him because He first loved me and gave His life for me. Now that I have been loved, I can love. No longer dependent totally on the external for affirmation, I am free to choose.

My vineyard is very costly and will not be given away cheaply by lending myself to less than committed covenant love. By choice my borders are enclosed, my spring shut up, my fountain sealed.

I am waiting patiently in Eden for my soul mate, the one chosen for me by God. My Adam will find me there, and as I am presented to him, he will leave and cleave unto me. The two of us shall marry in the sight of God to become covenanted together as one. Then as he stirs and awakens my love, I will open to him. He will go down into his garden that has been kept for him alone and feed among the beds of spices and lie all night between my breasts.

He will eat my honeycomb and drink of the spiced wine of the juice of my pomegranates, while his left hand is under my head and his right hand, embracing and caressing me. In the midst of love consummated and sacred intimacy explored, we will thank God for giving us this gift of the wonderment and mystifying beauty between a man and his wife.

Ahh yes, the winter is past; the flood rains are over and gone. Flowers have now appeared. The singing of the birds is at hand and the voice of the turtledove can distinctly be heard in our land. Fig trees are putting forth green figs and the vines, with tender grapes, are sending forth a heavenly aroma, a sweet fruitful fragrance. Indeed, heaven has come to kiss the earth, to give its approval of our love.

EPILOGUE 2

The Lamb-Hearted Lion

A portrait of a godly woman

"I have nothing to wear!" said Highly Favored as she browsed through her closet. Everything was faded, old, and boring.

"I need a complete make over. Something new and daring," she decided. *"I know what I'll do. I will go to my Father. He dresses the lilies of the field and has promised to clothe me with much more."*

Highly Favored came before the presence of her Father. *"Abba Father, I need some new clothes that will change the way I look,"* she informed Him. *"And I will wear whatever you choose for me."*

He smiled. Abba went to His heavenly closet and pulled out 1 Peter 3:4. It was not at all what she had hoped for. It was a modest white linen undergarment called Meek and Quiet Spirit. Highly Favored's heart sank. Her face changed to a look of disappointment.

"This is the undergarment of righteousness and humility," Abba informed her. *"You must wear it next to your heart at all times and learn to serve others before yourself."* Next, He pulled out Proverbs 31:25. It was a breathtakingly beautiful silk dress of diverse royal colors, a garment fit for a queen. It was called Strength and Honor.

"You are my princess," her Father stated, *"and must walk with the dignity befitting nobility."*

Highly Favored jumped with joy. *"Yes! This is what I had hoped for,"* she exclaimed with delight as she ran from His presence.

"I have much to accomplish," she said, *"but this ole scratchy petticoat will only hinder my plans."* Its drabness seemed multiplied in comparison to the brilliant splendor of the dress.

She cast the unimpressive undergarment aside as she looked at the grandeur of her gown.

"Now, I will get some respect and people will listen to what I have to say," she exclaimed confidently. Slipping into the dress, out she went into the marketplace adorned as a queen.

By the end of the day, however, she sat all alone. *"People are so stupid and stubborn,"* she insisted. *"And so very irritating and overly sensitive. They won't listen to me. If I were really a queen, I would command, 'off with their heads!'"*

As she sat there, the mirror reflected the ugliness and harshness of her thoughts. *"Oh,"* she cried. *"This is really not what I want to look like."* So, she took off her dress and put on her modest petticoat. *"Tomorrow I will stay in the background,"* she professed, *"quiet and hidden away at home. I won't go anywhere nor get involved in anything. I will just pray and give anonymously and sacrifice my life for the good of others."*

But again, by the end of the day, there she sat all alone, her head hanging down. *"It is so lonely here,"* she insisted. *"I am sacrificing, and no one notices or appreciates it. I'm like an old used shoe with no value or worth."*

She pulled off her petticoat. *"I have nothing to wear,"* she stated in defeat and slipped back into her old apparel, when the room suddenly brightened, almost like a lighthouse. And there stood an angel with his wings spread in majestic display.

"Highly Favored," he said gently but firmly. *"Take off that strange apparel. It is not befitting the king's children.*

"Look!" the angel said. *"It is the Lion of the tribe of Judah; the heir*

to David's throne, the One who has prevailed."

Highly Favored looked up from her state of despair, but instead of a Lion, there stood a Lamb in the midst of the throne as though it had been slain. His white garment hung down to the feet and girded about His chest was a golden band. He was clothed with strength and honor. On His robe it read, "King of kings," and on His head sat the crown of a king. Glory, honor, strength, and gladness were in His presence. Jesus held out His nail scared hands. His tender eyes pierced her very being with so much love that despair could not stay in His company.

The angel spoke. *"Daughter, your King comes to you as a Servant-King. Jesus is meek and lowly in heart. His strength is perfected through meekness; honor through quietness. The secret to the Kingdom is to first be adorned with the hidden undergarments of a Meek and Quiet Spirit, adding to that, the outer clothing of Strength and honor. When you learn to wear both simultaneously, you will know Him and be like Him in power and humility."*

Highly Favored fell at the feet of the one who loved her. *"Be it done unto me according to your word,"* she cried. Jesus clothed her with His heavenly raiment. The humble undergarment was now a comfort to her and caused the outer garment of Strength and Honor to be a perfect fit.

"You are a royal priesthood," Jesus said. *"I have made you to be both a queen and a servant. With the Lion's strength and the Lamb's meekness, you shall reign upon the earth. Now, go in peace, for I have given you power and authority over the challenges of life. Never forget, I will be with you always to help you become all that I have made you to be."*

And so Highly Favored began her journey to become a Lamb-hearted Lion and to learn to release the meekness of the Lamb and the boldness of the Lion at their proper times. Sometimes, however, there would be too much lion and she would roar with harshness and offend those around her. At other times, there was too much lamb and her shyness caused her to lose her identity and authority. But it was only a matter of time, as she chose to first put on her undergarment of a meek and gentle spirit, that peace began to rule her life. And through God's assistance, the Lion began to lie down with the Lamb and the character of Christ was seen through her in all of His glory.

ABOUT THE AUTHOR

Lornah Stump Nelson is co-founder of Camp Alandale, a nonprofit award-winning camp for abused and underprivileged kids, located in Alandale, California.

She was an entrepreneur and past owner of several businesses, both wholesale and retail, as well as an interior designer and creator and manufacturer of meaningful Kingdom Products.

Lornah was a speaker in the marketplace, as well as in churches and various Christian organizations such as Aglow and its annual Orange County conference.

She was also the founder and President of Women of Influence, an organization for women from all walks of life.

Lornah Stump is an author and teacher of the Word of God.

She is the creator of thelostcovenant.com website.

To contact her please do so on the website.

ENDNOTES

1 *Field of Dreams,* Directed by Phil Alden (1989; Universal City, CA; Universal Studios, 2006 DVD)
2 Michael L. Galiga, *Win Every Battle,* (Minn. MN: Bronze Bow Publishing, 2009) page 144
3 Jon and Joline Hamil, Lamplighter Ministries
4 Sean Feucht, Burn 24-7, Light a Candle, Hold the Line
5 Julie Smith, Elijahlist editor
6 Chuck Pierce, Glory of Zion International
7 Rick Warren, *The Purpose Driven Life,* (Grand Rapids Mich. USA: Zondervan, copyright 2002) Page 30
8 Dr Myles Munroe, *In Pursuit of Purpose,* (Shippensburg PA; Destiny Image, copyright 1992) preface and page 31,32
9 Mirriam Webster, Webster's New World Dictionary, (New York, New York, Simon and Schuster, 1984, page 3
10 James Strong, Strong's Exhaustive Concordance, (Nashville Tennessee: Thomas Nelson, 1995), ref.#7965, pg 142, ref.# 7451, pg 133
11 Bill Johnson, Senior Leader of Bethel Church, Redding, CA.
12 Bill Johnson, Senior Leader of Bethel Church, Redding, CA.
13 Mark Chironna, Lead Pastor, Church on the Living Edge, Longwood, Florida.
14 James Strong, Strong's Exhaustive Concordance, (Nashville Tennessee: Thomas Nelson, 1995), ref # 3296 Heb., pg 56, # 3813 Grk., pg 66, # 1121 Heb., pg 1121, # 5707 Grk. Pg 93.
15 John Courson , Application Commentary New Testament, (Nashville, Tennessee, Thomas Nelson, copy-

right 2003) pag 74

16 Bill Johnson, Senior Leader of Bethel Church, Redding, CA.

17 Jeff Wittmer, Destiny Builders Workshop

18 Bill Winston, *The Blessing Collection; Commanding the Blessing*, DVD series, (Bill Winston Ministries, Oak Park ILL.) copyright 2016

19 Brian Simmons, Passion Bible, *John Eternal Love,* (Racine, WI., Broadstreet Publishing Group LLC, copyright 2014) pg 23

20 Graham Cooke, Founder of Brilliant Perspectives

21 Kathi Pelton, Inscribe Ministries

22 Unknown source

23 Kris Vallotton, Senior Associate Leader at Bethel Church, Redding CA.

24 Jennifer Eivaz, Executive Pastor, Harvest Church, Turlock, CA.

25 John Eldredge, *Wild at Heart*, (Nashville TN.: Thomas Nelson Publishers, copyright 2001) Chapter 9, page 17

26 David Wilkerson, Founding Pastor of Times Square Church, New York City, NY.

27 Graham Cooke, *Crafted Prayer,* (Vancouver WA., Brilliant Book House, copyright 2015) Appendix 1

28 Dead Sea Scrolls, 11Q13, Column 2

29 Alan Vincent, Outpouring Ministries

30 Graham Cooke, *Crafted Prayer,* (Vancouver WA., Brilliant Book House, copyright 2015) Appendix 1

31 James Strong, Strong's Exhaustive Concordance, (Nashville Tennessee: Thomas Nelson, 1995), Ref. # 4043 Heb., pg 72

32 James Strong, Strong's Exhaustive Concordance, (Nashville Tennessee: Thomas Nelson, 1995), Ref. # 5674 Heb., pg 102, #6452 Heb., pg 115

33 Josephus Antiquities 2.16.1

34 Josephus Antiquities 2.16.1

35 Josephus Antiquities 2.16.2

36 James Strong, Strong's Exhaustive Concordance, (Nashville Tennessee: Thomas Nelson, 1995), Ref.# 4991 Grk., pg 88

37 Graham Cooke, Crafted Prayer, Appendix 1

38 Graham Cooke, Crafted Prayer, Pg 3, 20, 21,

39 Josephus Antiquities 2.16.2

40 Graham Cooke Graham, *Crafted Prayer,* (Vancouver WA., Brilliant Book House, copyright 2015) Appendix 1

41 James Strong, Strong's Exhaustive Concordance, (Nashville Tennessee: Thomas Nelson, 1995), Ref. # 7939 Heb., pg 142

42 Josephus Book VI, Chapter 2

43 Josephus Book VI, Chapter 3

44 Josephus Book VI, Chapter 3

45 Josephus Book of Antiquities

46 Dallas Willard, *The Divine Conspiracy,* (San Francisco CA., Harper Collins Publishers, copyright 1966) pg 15

47 Dr Myles Munroe, Founder of Bahamas Faith Ministries International, Nassau, Bahamas

48 Bill Winston, Create Your Future

49 Graham Cooke, *Crafted Prayer,* (Vancouver WA., Brilliant Book House, copyright 2015) Appendix 1

50 Eric Johnson, Senior Pastor, Bethel Church, Redding CA.

51 Israel Ministry of Foreign Affairs

52 James Strong, Strong's Exhaustive Concordance, (Nashville Tennessee: Thomas Nelson, 1995), Ref. # 4160 Grk, pg 72-73, # 1096 Grk., pg 19

53 James Strong, Strong's Exhaustive Concordance, (Nashville Tennessee: Thomas Nelson, 1995), Ref. # 3341 Grk., pg 57

54 Dallas Willard, *The Divine Conspiracy,* (San Francisco CA., Harper Collins Publishers, copyright 1966) pg

30,31

55 Graham Cooke, *Crafted Prayer,* (Vancouver WA., Brilliant Book House, copyrite 2015) Appendix 1

56 James Strong, Strong's Exhaustive Concordance, (Nashville Tennessee: Thomas Nelson, 1995), Ref. # 5219, Grk., pg 93, # 5091 Grk., pg 90

57 Forest Gump movie, Robert Zemeckis, Tom Hanks, (1994, Paramount Pictures, Los Angeles, CA.)

58 Graham Cooke, Day One, "Do you believe what God believes about you?"

59 James Strong, Strong's Exhaustive Concordance, (Nashville Tennessee: Thomas Nelson, 1995), Ref. # 87 Heb., pg 2, # 85 Heb., pg 2

60 James Strong, Strong's Exhaustive Concordance, (Nashville Tennessee: Thomas Nelson, 1995), Ref. # 8297 Heb., pg 148, # 8283 Heb., pg 148

61 Graham Cooke, *Crafted Prayer,* (Vancouver WA., Brilliant Book House, copyright 2015) Appendix 1

62 James Strong, Strong's Exhaustive Concordance, (Nashville Tennessee: Thomas Nelson, 1995), Ref. # 2644 Grk., pg 47

63 Graham Cooke, *Crafted Prayer,* (Vancouver WA., Brilliant Book House, copyright 2015) Appendix 1

64 President Trump, Trending Politics

65 Graham Cooke, *Crafted Prayer,* (Vancouver WA., Brilliant Book House, copyright 2015) Appendix 1

66 James Strong, Strong's Exhaustive Concordance, (Nashville Tennessee: Thomas Nelson, 1995), Ref. # 34 Heb., pg 1

67 James Strong, Strong's Exhaustive Concordance, (Nashville Tennessee: Thomas Nelson, 1995), Ref., # 5157, Heb., pg 92, #3678 Heb., pg 65

68 James Strong, Strong's Exhaustive Concordance, (Nashville Tennessee: Thomas Nelson, 1995), Ref. # 3427 Heb., pg 60

69 James Strong, Strong's Exhaustive Concordance,

(Nashville Tennessee: Thomas Nelson, 1995), Ref. # 7965 Heb., pg 142

70 James Strong, Strong's Exhaustive Concordance, (Nashville Tennessee: Thomas Nelson, 1995), Ref. # 4369 Grk., pg 77

71 Kent Christmas, Regeneration Church, (Nashville Tennessee; Podcast

72 James Strong, Strong's Exhaustive Concordance, (Nashville Tennessee: Thomas Nelson, 1995), Ref. # 3812 Heb., pg 68

73 James Strong, Strong's Exhaustive Concordance, (Nashville Tennessee: Thomas Nelson, 1995), Ref. # 3063 Heb., pg 54

74 Brown Driver Briggs Hebrew and English Lexacon, copyright2002, Hendrickson publisher

75 Bill Johnson, An Important Update from Bethel Leadership, 11/22/20

CPSIA information can be obtained
at www.ICGtesting.com
Printed in the USA
LVHW021622280521
688802LV00017B/558

Covenant empowers you to prevail in chaotic times and have peace in the midst of storms.

What is Covenant? Why do I need it? Covenant is about Jesus. It's not about what you can do for Him, but what He wants to do in and through you. In Covenant, you'll experience new adventures and have greater intimacy with the Trinity. Covenant connects you to God's purpose for your life and answers questions like: "Why was I born? Who is God for me alone? And who am I?"

You'll move from a normal life into a supernatural one; from who you once were, to who you really are; from 'I was,' to 'I am.' The past will no longer define the present. Covenant doesn't prevent suffering or hardships but overcomes them. You'll begin to think and pray like a son and heir, instead of a servant. You'll learn to stop struggling in your own efforts and step into what Jesus is doing.

As a Covenant Heir of God, you will discover:

- The promised birthrights, blessings, and resources that belong to the family of God.
- How to access Abraham's blessings that are included in the New Covenant.
- Covenant is the secret to winning every battle.
- Covenant and the Kingdom of God are intertwined and equally important.

Lornah Stump spent seventeen years pursuing revelation of covenant and living it with life changing results. She was on staff at a Spirit-filled church as a teacher, speaker, and mentor to women. Lornah went from a difficult past of wishing she had never been born to finding covenant and the purpose of her birth. Her mundane life turned into realized potential. She began living a grand adventure discovering secret riches and treasures hidden in dark places. Her personal experiences will convince you that Covenant is indeed worthy of your focus and will fill you with awe.